LIBRARY

OF

ABORIGINAL AMERICAN

LITERATURE.

No. VII.

EDITED BY

D. G. BRINTON

BRINTON'S LIBRARY OF
ABORIGINAL AMERICAN LITERATURE.
NUMBER VII.

ANCIENT
NAHUATL POETRY,

CONTAINING THE NAHUATL TEXT OF XXVII ANCIENT
MEXICAN POEMS.

WITH A TRANSLATION, INTRODUCTION, NOTES AND
VOCABULARY.

BY

DANIEL G. BRINTON

AMS PRESS
NEW YORK

Reprinted from the edition of 1890, Philadelphia
First AMS EDITION published 1969
Manufactured in the United States of America

Library of Congress Catalogue Card Number: 70-83462

AMS PRESS, INC.
New York, N.Y. 10003

PREFACE.

It is with some hesitation that I offer this volume to the scientific public. The text of the ancient songs which it contains offers extreme and peculiar difficulties to the translator, and I have been obliged to pursue the task without assistance of any kind. Not a line of them has ever before been rendered into an European tongue, and my endeavors to obtain aid from some of the Nahuatl scholars of Mexico have, for various reasons, proved ineffectual. I am therefore alone responsible for errors and misunderstandings.

Nevertheless, I have felt that these monuments of ancient native literature are so interesting in themselves, and so worthy of publication, that they should be placed at the disposition of scholars in their original form with the best rendering that I could give them at present, rather than to await the uncertain event of years for a better.

The text itself may be improved by comparison with the original MS. and with the copy previously made by the Licentiate Chimalpopoca, referred to on page 48. My own efforts in this direction have been confined to a faithful reproduction in print of the MS. copy of the Abbé Brasseur de Bourbourg.

The Notes, which might easily have been extended, I

have confined within moderate compass, so as not to enlarge unduly the bulk of the volume.

To some, the Vocabulary may seem inadequate. I assume that those persons who wish to make a critical study of the original text will provide themselves with the Nahuatl Dictionaries of Molina or Siméon, both of which are now easily obtainable, thanks to Mr. Julius Platzmann for the reprint of Molina. I also assume that such students will acquaint themselves with the rules of grammar and laws of word-building of the tongue, and that they will use the vocabulary merely as a labor-saving means of reaching the themes of compounds and unusual forms of words. Employed in this manner, it will, I hope, be found adequate.

In conclusion, I would mention that there is a large body of Nahuatl literature yet unpublished, both prose and poetry, modern and ancient, and as the Nahuatl tongue is one of the most highly developed on the American continent, it is greatly to be desired that all this material should be at the command of students. The Nahuatl, moreover, is not a difficult tongue; for an Englishman or a Frenchman, I should say it is easier to acquire than German, its grammar being simple and regular, and its sounds soft and sonorous. It has special recommendations, therefore, to one who would acquaint himself with an American language.

CONTENTS.

ANCIENT

NAHUATL POETRY.

INTRODUCTION.

§ 1. *The National Love of Poetry.*

The passionate love with which the Nahuas cultivated song, music and the dance is a subject of frequent comment by the historians of Mexico. These arts are invariably mentioned as prominent features of the aboriginal civilization; no public ceremony was complete without them; they were indispensable in the religious services held in the temples; through their assistance the sacred and historical traditions were preserved; and the entertainments of individuals received their chief lustre and charm from their association with these arts.

The profession of the poet stood in highest honor. It was the custom before the Conquest for every town, every ruler and every person of importance to maintain a company of singers and dancers, paying them fixed salaries, and the early writer, Duran, tells us that this custom continued in his own time, long after the Conquest. He sensibly adds, that he can see nothing improper in it, although it was condemned by some of the Spaniards.[1] In the training of these artists their patrons took a deep personal interest, and were not at all tolerant of neglected duties. We are told that the chief selected the song which was to be sung, and the tune by which it was to be accompanied; and did any one of the choir sing falsely, a drummer beat out of time, or a dancer strike an incorrect attitude, the unfortunate artist was instantly called forth, placed in bonds and summarily executed the next morning![2]

With critics of such severity to please, no wonder that it was necessary to begin the training early, and to set apart for it definite places and regular teachers. Therefore it was one of the established duties of the teachers in the *calmecac* or public school, "to teach the pupils all the verses of the sacred songs which were written in characters in their books."[3] There were also special schools, called *cuicoyan*, singing places, where both sexes were taught to sing the popular songs and to dance to the sound of the drums.[4] In the public ceremonies it was no uncommon occurrence for

---

[1] Diego Duran, *Historia de las Indias de Nueva España*, Tom. I, p. 233; and compare Geronimo de Mendieta, *Historia Eclesiastica Indiana*, Lib. II, cap. 31.

[2] Sahagun, *Historia de Nueva España*, Lib. VIII, cap. 26.

[3] Sahagun, *Historia de Nueva España*, Lib. III, cap. 8.

[4] *Cuicoyan*, from *cuica*, song, and the place-ending *yan*, which is added to the impersonal form of the verb, in this instance, *cuicoa*. Mr. Bancroft entirely misapprehends Tezozomoc's words about these establishments, and gives an erroneous rendering of the term. See his *Native Races of the Pacific Coast*, Vol. II, p. 290, and Tezozomoc, *Cronica Mexicana*, cap. 18.

the audience to join in the song and dance until sometimes many thousands would thus be seized with the contagion of the rhythmical motion, and pass hours intoxicated (to use a favorite expression of the Nahuatl poets) with the cadence and the movement.

After the Conquest the Church set its face firmly against the continuance of these amusements. Few of the priests had the liberal views of Father Duran, already quoted; most of them were of the opinion of Torquemada, who urges the clergy " to forbid the singing of the ancient songs, because all of them are full of idolatrous memories, or of diabolical and suspicious allusions of the same character." [1]

To take the place of the older melodies, the natives were taught the use of the musical instruments introduced by the Spaniards, and very soon acquired no little proficiency, so that they could perform upon them, compose original pieces, and manufacture most of the instruments themselves. [2]

To this day the old love of the song and dance continues in the Indian villages; and though the themes are changed, the forms remain with little alteration. Travelers describe the movements as slow, and consisting more in bending and swaying the body than in motions of the feet; while the

---

[1] Juan de Torquemada, *Monarquia Indiana*, Lib. VI, cap. 43.

[2] Torquemada, *Monarquia Indiana*, Lib. XVII, cap. 3. Didacus Valades, who was in Mexico about 1550, writes of the natives : " Habent instrumenta musica permulta in quibus æmulatione quadam se exercent." *Rhetorica Christiana*, Pars. IV, cap. 24.

songs chanted either refer to some saint or biblical character, or are erotic and pave the way to orgies.[1]

§ 2. *The Poet and his Work.*

The Nahuatl word for a song or poem is *cuicatl.* It is
derived from the verb *cuica,* to sing, a term probably imi-
tative or onomatopoietic in origin, as it is also a general
expression for the twittering of birds. The singer was
called *cuicani,* and is distinguished from the composer of
the song, the poet, to whom was applied the term *cuicapicqui,*
in which compound the last member, *picqui,* corresponds
strictly to the Greek ποιητής, being a derivative of *piqui,* to
make, to create.[2] Sometimes he was also called *cuica-
tlamantini,* "skilled in song."

It is evident from these words, all of which belong to the
ancient language, that the distinction between the one who
composed the poems and those who sang them was well
established, and that the Nahuatl poetry was, therefore,
something much above mere improvisation, as some have
thought. This does not alter the fact that a professed
bard usually sang songs of his own composition, as well
as those obtained from other sources. This is obvious from
the songs in this collection, many of which contain the
expression *ni cuicani,* I, the singer, which also refers to the
maker of the song.

---

[1] Descriptions are given by Edward Mühlenpfordt, *Die Republik Mexico,*
Bd. I, pp. 250–52 (Hannover, 1844).

[2] Molina translates *piqui,* "crear ô plasmar Dios alguna cosa de
nuevo." *Vocabulario de la Lengua Mexicana,* s. v.

In the classical work of Sahagun, the author describes the ancient poet: "The worthy singer has a clear mind and a strong memory. He composes songs himself and learns those of others, and is always ready to impart either to the fellows of his craft. He sings with a well-trained voice, and is careful to practice in private before he appears before the public. The unworthy singer, on the other hand, is ignorant and indolent. What he learns he will not communicate to others. His voice is hoarse and untrained, and he is at once envious and boastful."[1]

§ 3. *The Themes and Classes of the Songs.*

From what he could learn about them some two centuries or more after the Conquest, the antiquary Boturini classified all the ancient songs under two general heads, the one treating mainly of historical themes, while the other was devoted to purely fictitious, emotional or imaginative subjects.[2] His terse classification is expanded by the Abbé Clavigero, who states that the themes of the ancient poets were various, some chanting the praises of the gods or petitioning them for favors, others recalled the history of former generations, others were didactic and inculcated correct habits of life, while others, finally, were in lighter vein, treating of hunting, games and love.[3]

His remarks were probably a generalization from a chapter in Torquemada's *Monarquia Indiana,* in which that writer

---

[1] Sahagun, *Historia de Nueva España,* Lib. X, cap. 8.

[2] Boturini, *Idea de una Nueva Historia General,* p. 97.

[3] Clavigero, *Storia antica di Messico,* Lib. VII, p. 175.

states that the songs at the sacred festivals differed in subject with the different months and seasons. Thus, in the second month of their calendar, at its stated festival, the people sang the greatness of their rulers; in the seventh month all the songs were of love, of women, or of hunting; in the eighth the chants recalled the noble deeds of their ancestors and their divine origin; while in the ninth month nothing was heard but verses fraught with lamentation for the dead.[1] With less minuteness, Father Duran gives almost the same information. He himself had often heard the songs which Montezuma of Tenochtitlan, and Nezahualpizintli of Tezcuco, had ordered to be composed in their own honor, describing their noble lineage, their riches, their grandeur and their victories. These songs were in his day still sung at the public dances of the natives, and he adds, "although they were filled with laudation of their ancient rulers, it gave me much pleasure to hear the praises of such grandeur." There were other poets, he observes, who lived in the temples and composed songs exclusively in honor of the gods.[2]

These general expressions may be supplemented by a list of terms, specifying particular classes of songs, preserved by various writers. These are as follows:—

melahuacuicatl: this is translated by Tezozomoc, "a straight and true song."[3] It is a compound of *melahuac,* straight, direct, true; and *cuicatl,* song. It was a begin-

---

[1] Torquemada, *Monarquia Indiana,* Lib. X, cap. 34.

[2] Duran, *Hist. de la Indias de Nueva España,* Tom. I, p. 233.

[3] Tezozomoc, *Cronica Mexicana,* cap. 64.

ning or opening song at the festivals, and apparently derived its name from its greater intelligibility and directness of expression.   A synonym, derived from the same root, is *tlamelauhcayotl*, which appears in the title to some of the songs in the present collection.

xopancuicatl: this term is spelled by Ixtlilxochitl, *xompacuicatl*, and explained to mean "a song of the spring" (from *xopan*, springtime, *cuicatl*, song).   The expression seems to be figurative, referring to the beginning or early life of things.   Thus, the prophetic songs of Nezahualcoyotl, those which he sang when he laid the foundation of his great palace, bore this name.[1]

teuccuicatl: songs of the nobles (*teuctli, cuicatl*).   These were also called *quauhcuicatl*, "eagle songs," the term *quauhtli*, eagle, being applied to distinguished persons.

xochicuicatl: flower-song, one singing the praises of flowers.

icnocuicatl: song of destitution or compassion.

noteuhcuicaliztli: "the song of my lords."   This appears to be a synonymous expression for *teuccuicatl;* it is mentioned by Boturini, who adds that on the day sacred to the god Xiuhteuctli the king began the song so called.[2]

miccacuicatl: the song for the dead (*miqui*, to die, *cuicatl*).   In this solemn chant the singers were seated on the ground, and their hair was twisted in plaits around their heads.[3]

---

[1] Ixtlilxochitl, *Historia Chichimeca*, cap. 47.

[2] Boturini, *Idea de una Nueva Historia General*, p. 90.

[3] Tezozomoc, *Cronica Mexicana*, cap. 53.

In addition to the above terms drawn from the subject or character of the songs, there were others, of geographical origin, apparently indicating that the song, or its tune, or its treatment was borrowed from another locality or people.   These are:—

Huexotzincayotl: a song of Huexotzinco, a Nahuatl town, situate east of the Lake of Tezcuco. This song was sung by the king and superior nobles at certain festivals, and, in the prescribed order of the chants, followed a *melahuac-cuicatl*.[1]

Chalcayotl: a song of Chalco, on the lake of the same name. This followed the last mentioned in order of time at the festivals.

Otoncuicatl: a song of the Otomis. These were the immediate neighbors of the Nahuas, but spoke a language radically diverse. The songs so-called were sung fourth on the list.

Cuextecayotl: a song of the country of the Cuexteca, or Cuextlan, a northern province of Mexico.

Tlauancacuextecayotl: a song of the country of the Tlauancacuexteca.

Anahuacayotl: a song of Anahuac, that is, of a country near the water, either the valley of Mexico, or the shores of the ocean.

Some very ancient sacred songs were referred to by Tezozomoc as peculiar to the worship of Huitzilopochtli, and, indeed, introduced by this potent divinity.   From

---

[1] See Sahagun, *Historia de Neuva España*, Lib. IV, chap. 17, and Tezozomoc, *Cronica Mexicana*, cap. 64.

their names, *cuitlaxoteyotl*, and *tecuilhuicuicatl*,[1] I judge
that they referred to some of those pederastic rites which
still prevail extensively among the natives of the pueblos
of New Mexico, and which have been described by Dr.
William A. Hammond and other observers.[2] One of these
songs began,

Cuicoyan	nohuan	mitotia ;
In-the-place-of-song	with-me	they-dance.

But the old chronicler, who doubtless knew it all by
heart, gives us no more of it.[3]

§ 4. *Prosody of the Songs.*

The assertion is advanced by Boturini that the genuine ancient Nahuatl poetry which has been preserved is
in iambic metre, and he refers to a song of Nezahualcoyotl in his collection to prove his opinion. What study
I have given to the prosody of the Nahuatl tongue leads
me to doubt the correctness of so sweeping a statement.
The vocalic elements of the language have certain peculiarities which prevent its poetry from entering unencum-
bered into the domain of classical prosody.

The quantity of Nahuatl syllables is a very important
element in the pronunciation of the tongue, but their
quantity is not confined, as in Latin, to long, short, and

---

[1] *Cuitlaxoteyotl*, from *cuitatl*, mierda; *tecuilhuicuicatl*, from *tecuil-
huaztli*, sello, *tecuilonti*, el que lo haze a otro, pecando contra natura.
Molina, *Vocabulario*.

[2] William A. Hammond, *The Disease of the Scythians* (*morbus femi-
narum*) *and Certain Analogous Conditions*, in the *American Journal of
Neurology and Psychiatry*, 1882.   [3] *Cronica Mexicana*, cap. 2.

common. The Nahuatl vowels are long, short, intermediate, and "with stress," or as the Spanish grammarians say, "with a jump," *con saltillo.* The last mentioned is peculiar to this tongue. The vowel so designated is pronounced with a momentary suspension or catching of the breath, rendering it emphatic.

These quantities are prominent features in the formal portions of the language, characterizing inflections and declinations. No common means of designating them have been adopted by the grammarians, and for my present purpose, I shall make use of the following signs:—

ă , short.

a , intermediate.

ā , long.

â , with stress.

The general prosodic rules are :—

1. In polysyllabic words in which there are no long vowels, all the vowels are intermediate.

2. The vowels are long in the penultimate of the plurals of the imperatives when the preterit of the verb ends in a vowel; the *ā* of the *cān* of the imperatives; the *ī* of the *tī* of the gerundives; the last vowel of the futures when the verb loses a vowel to form them; the penultimates of passives in *lo*, of impersonals, of verbals in *oni, illi, olli* and *oca*, of verbal nouns with the terminations *yan* and *can;* the ō of abstract nouns in *otl* in composition; and those derived from long syllables.

3. Vowels are "with stress" when they are the finals in the plurals of nouns and verbs, also in the perfect preterite, in possessives ending in â, ê, ô, and in the penul-

timate of nouns ending in *tli, tla* and *tle* when these syllables are immediately preceded by the vowel.[1]

The practical importance of these distinctions may be illustrated by the following examples :—

>   *tâtli* , = father.
>   *tātlī* , = thou drinkest.
>   *tātlî* , = we drink.

It is, however, evident from this example that the quantity of Nahuatl syllables enters too much into the strictly formal part of the language for rules of position, such as some of those above given, to be binding; and doubtless for this reason the eminent grammarian Carlos de Tapia Zenteno, who was professor of the tongue in the University of Mexico, denies that it can be reduced to definite rules of prosody like those of the Latin.[2]

Substituting accent for quantity, there would seem to be an iambic character to the songs. Thus the first words of Song I, were probably chanted :—

>   *Nino' yolno' notza' campa' nicŭ iz' yec tli' ahui aca' xochitl'* :
> etc.

---

[1] On this subject the reader may consult Paredes, *Compendio del Arte de la Lengua Mexicana*, pp. 5, 6, and Sandoval, *Arte de la Lengua Mexicana*, pp. 60, 61. Tapia Zenteno whose *Arte Novissima de la Lengua Mexicana* was published in 1753, rejects altogether the saltillo, and says its invention is of no use except to make students work harder ! (pp. 3, 4.) The vowels with saltillo, he maintains, are simply to be pronounced with a slight aspiration. Nevertheless, the late writers continue to employ and describe the saltillo, as Chimalpopoca, *Epitome ó Modo Fácil de aprender el Idioma Nahuatl*, p. 6. (Mexico, 1869.)

[2] *Arte Novissima de la Lengua Mexicana*, pp. 3, 4.

But the directions given for the drums at the beginning of Songs XVIII, XIX, etc., do not indicate a continuance of these feet, but of others, as in XIX:—

$$\cup- , \cup- , \cup- , \cup\cup- , \cup- , \cup- , \cup-, \text{etc.}$$

Indeed, we may suppose that the metre varied with the subject and the skill of the poet. This, in fact, is the precise statement of Father Duran,[1] who speaks of the native poets as "giving to each song a different tune (*sonada*), as we are accustomed in our poetry to have the sonnet, the octava rima and the terceto."

§ 5. *The Vocal Delivery of the Song.*

Descriptions of the concerts so popular among the Nahuas have been preserved by the older writers, and it is of the highest importance to understand their methods in order to appreciate the songs presented in this volume.

These concerts were held on ceremonial occasions in the open air, in the village squares or in the courtyards of the houses. They began in the morning and usually continued until nightfall, occasionally far into the night. The musicians occupied the centre of the square and the trained singers stood or sat around them. When the sign was given to begin, the two most skillful singers, sometimes a man and a woman, pronounced the first syllables of the song slowly but with a sharp emphasis;[2] then the drums began in a low tone, and gradually increased in

---

[1] Duran, *Historia de Nueva España*, Tom. I, p. 230.

[2] The singer who began the song was called *cuicaito*, "the speaker of the song."

strength as the song proceeded; the other singers united their voices until the whole chorus was in action, and often the bystanders, to the numbers of thousands, would ultimately join in the words of some familiar song, keeping time by concerted movements of the hands and feet.

Each verse or couplet of the song was repeated three or four times before proceeding to the next, and those songs which were of the slowest measure and least emotional in character were selected for the earlier hours of the festivals. None of the songs was lengthy, even the longest, in spite of the repetitions, rarely lasting over an hour.[1]

The tone in which the words were chanted is described by Clavigero, Mühlenpfordt and other comparatively recent travelers as harsh, strident and disagreeable to the European ear. Mendieta calls it a "contra-bass," and states that persons gifted with such a voice cultivated it assiduously and were in great demand. The Nahuas call it *tozquitl*, the singing voice, and likened it to the notes of sweet singing birds.

§ 6. *The Instrumental Accompaniment.*

The Nahuas were not acquainted with any stringed instrument. They manufactured, however, a variety of objects from which they could extract what seemed to them melodious sounds. The most important were two forms of drums, the *huehuetl* and the *teponaztli*.

---

[1] The most satisfactory description of these concerts is that given by Geronimo de Mendieta, *Historia Eclesiastica Indiana*, Lib. II, cap. 31. I have taken some particulars from Boturini and Sahagun.

The word *huehuetl* means something old, something ancient, and therefore important and great. The drum so-called was a hollow cylinder of wood, thicker than a man's body, and usually about five palms in height. The end was covered with tanned deerskin, firmly stretched. The sides were often elaborately carved and tastefully painted. This drum was placed upright on a stand in front of the player and the notes were produced by striking the parchment with the tips of the fingers.

A smaller variety of this instrument was called *tlapanhuehuetl*, or the half drum, which was of the same diameter but only half the height.[1] Still another variety was the *yopihuehuetl*, "the drum which tears out the heart,"[2] so called either by reason of its penetrating and powerful sound, or because it was employed at the *Yopico*, where that form of human sacrifice was conducted.

The *teponaztli* was a cylindrical block of wood hollowed out below, and on its upper surface with two longitudinal parallel grooves running nearly from end to end, and a third in the centre at right angles to these, something in the shape of the letter ⲓ. The two tongues left between the grooves were struck with balls of rubber, *ulli*, on the ends of handles or drum sticks. These instruments varied greatly

---

[1] Literally, "the broken drum," from *tlapana*, to break, as they say *tlapanhuimetzli*, half moon. It is described by Tezozomoc as "un atambor bajo." *Cronica Mexicana*, cap. 53.

[2] From *yollotl*, heart, and *pi*, to tear out. The instrument is mentioned by Tezozomoc, *Cronica Mexicana*, cap. 48. On the Yopico, and its ceremonies, see Sahagun, *Historia de Nueva España*, Lib. II, cap. 1, and Appendix.

in size, some being five feet in length, and others so small that they could conveniently be carried suspended to the neck. The *teponaztli* was the house instrument of the Nahuas. It was played in the women's apartments to amuse the noble ladies, and the war captains carried one at the side to call the attention of their cohorts on the field of battle (Sahagun). The word is derived from the name of the tree whose wood was selected to make the drum, and this in turn from the verb *teponazoa*, to swell, probably from some peculiarity of its growth.[1]

A much superior instrument to the teponaztli, and doubtless a development from it, was the *tecomapiloa*, "the suspended vase" (*tecomatl*, gourd or vase, *piloa*, to hang or suspend). It was a solid block of wood, with a projecting ridge on its upper surface and another opposite, on its lower aspect ; to the latter one or more gourds or vases were suspended, which increased and softened the sound when the upper ridge was struck with the *ulli*.[2] This was undoubtedly the origin of the *marimba*, which I have described elsewhere.[3]

---

[1] Simeon, however, thinks the name arose from the growing and swelling of the sound of the instrument (notes to Jourdanet's translation of Sahagun, p. 28). Mr. H. H. Bancroft gives the astonishing translation of teponaztli, " wing of stone vapor !" (*Native Races of the Pacific States*, Vol. II, p. 293.) Brasseur traced the word to a Maya-Quiche root, *tep*. In both Nahuatl and Maya this syllable is the radicle of various words meaning to increase, enlarge, to grow strong or great, etc.

[2] Sahagun, *Hist. de Nueva España*, Lib. II, cap. 27.

[3] See *The Güegüence, a Comedy ballet in the Nahuatl Spanish dialect of Nicaragua*, Introd., p. 29. (Philadelphia, 1883.)

The musical properties of these drums have been discussed by Theodor Baker. The teponaztli, he states, could yield but two notes, and could not have been played in accord with the huehuetl. It served as an imperfect contra-bass. [1]

The *omichicahuaz*, "strong bone," was constructed somewhat on the principle of a *teponaztli*. A large and long bone was selected, as the femur of a man or deer, and it was channeled by deep longitudinal incisions. The projections left between the fissures were rasped with another bone or a shell, and thus a harsh but varied sound could be produced. [2]

The *tetzilacatl*, the "vibrator" or "resounder," was a sheet of copper suspended by a cord, which was struck with sticks or with the hand. It appears to have been principally confined to the sacred music in the temples.

The *ayacachtli* was a rattle formed of a jar of earthenware or a dried gourd containing pebbles which was fastened to a handle, and served to mark time in the songs and dances. An extension of this simple instrument was the *ayacachicahualiztli*, "the arrangement of rattles," which was a thin board about six feet long and

---

[1] Theodor Baker, *Ueber die Musik der Nord-Amerikanischen Wilden.*, pp. 51–53. (Leipzig, 1882.)

[2] *Omitl*, bone, *chicahuac*, strong. A specimen made of the bone of a fossil elephant is possessed by Señor A. Chavero, of Mexico. See Tezozomoc, *Cronica Mexicana*, cap. 55, and the note of Orozco y Berra to that passage in the Mexican edition. Also Sahagun, *Hist. de Nueva España*, Lib. VIII, cap. 20, who likewise describes most of the instruments referred to in this section.

a span wide, to which were attached bells, rattles and cylin drical pieces of hard wood. Shaking this produced a jingle-jangle, agreeable to the native ear. The Aztec bells of copper, *tzilinilli*, are really metallic rattles, like our sleigh bells. They are often seen in collections of Mexican antiquities. Other names for them were *coyolli* and *yoyotli*.

Various forms of flutes and fifes, made of reeds, of bone or of pottery, were called by names derived from the word *pitzaua*, to blow (e.g., *tlapitzalli*, *uilacapitzli*), and sometimes, as being punctured with holes, *zozoloctli*, from *zotl*, the awl or instrument used in perforating skins, etc. Many of those made of earthenware have been preserved, and they appear to have been a highly-esteemed instrument, as Sahagun mentions that the leader of the choir of singers in the temple bore the title *tlapitzcatzin*, "the noble flute player."

Large conches were obtained on the seashore and framed into wind instruments called *quiquiztli* and *tecciztli*, whose hoarse notes could be heard for long distances, and whistles of wood, bone and earthenware added their shrill notes to the noise of the chanting of the singers. The shell of the tortoise, *ayotl*, dried and suspended, was beaten in unison with such instruments.

Recent researches by competent musical experts conducted upon authentic specimens of the ancient Mexican instruments have tended to elevate our opinion of their skill in this art. Mr. H. T. Cresson, of the Academy of Natural Sciences, Philadelphia, has critically examined the various Aztec clay flutes, whistles, etc., which are there preserved, and has reached the following conclusions:—

c

"I. That upon the four-holed clay flageolets the chromatic and diatonic scales can be produced with a full octave.

"II. That the clay whistles or pitch pipes, which may be manipulated in quartette, will produce an octave and a fourth.

"III. From the facts above shown, the Aztecs must have possessed a knowledge of the scales as known to us, which has been fully tested by comparison with the flute and organ."[1]

This result indicates for the instrumental accompaniment a much higher position in musical notation than has hitherto been accepted.

§ 7. *The Poetic Dialect.*

All the old writers who were familiar with the native songs speak of their extreme obscurity, and the difficulty of translating them. No one will question the intimate acquaintance with the Nahuatl language possessed by Father Sahagun; yet no one has expressed more strongly than he the vagueness of the Nahuatl poetic dialect. "Our enemy on earth," he writes, "has prepared a thick woods and a dangerous ground full of pitfalls, wherein to devise his evil deeds and to hide himself from attack, as do wild beasts and venomous serpents. This woods and these pitfalls are the songs which he has inspired to be used in his service, as praises to his honor, in the temples and elsewhere; because they are composed with such a trick that

---

[1] H. T. Cresson, *On Aztec Music*, in the *Proceedings of the Academy of Natural Sciences, Philadelphia*, 1883.

they proclaim only what the devil commands, and are understood only by those to whom they are addressed. It is well known that the cavern, woods or depths in which the devil hides himself were these chants or psalms which he himself has composed, and which cannot be understood in their true significance except by those who are accustomed to the peculiar style of their language."[1]

Not less positive are the expressions of Father Diego Duran, contemporary of Sahagun, and himself well versed in the native tongue. "All their songs," he observes, "were composed in such obscure metaphors that scarcely any one can understand them unless he give especial attention to their construction."[2] The worthy Boturini was puzzled by those which he had collected, and writes, "the songs are difficult to explain, because they mystify historical facts with constant allegorizing,"[3] and Boturini's literary executor, Don Mariano Echevarria y Veitia, who paid especial attention to the poetic fragments he had received, says frankly: "The fact is, that as to the songs I have not found a person who can fully translate them, because there are many words in them whose signification is absolutely unknown to-day, and moreover which do not appear in the vocabularies of Molina or others."[4]

The Abbé Clavigero speaks in somewhat more definite

---

[1] Sahagun, *Historia de Nueva España*, Lib. II, Appendice.

[2] Duran, *Historia de las Indias de Nueva España*, Tom. I, p. 233.

[3] Boturini, *Idea de una Nueva Historia General*, Appendice, p. 95.

[4] Echevarria, *Historia del Origen de las Gentes de Nueva España*, Discurso Preliminar.

terms of the poetic forms and licenses of the language. He notes that in the fragments of the ancient verses which had been preserved until his day there were inserted between the significant words certain interjections and meaningless syllables, apparently to fill out the metre. Nevertheless, he considered the language of the chants, "pure, pleasant, brilliant, figurative and replete with allusions to the more pleasing objects in nature, as flowers, trees, brooks, etc."[1]

It is quite evident from the above extracts that in the translation of the ancient songs in the present volume we must be prepared for serious difficulties, the more so as the Nahuatl language, in the opinion of some who are the best acquainted with it, lends itself with peculiar facility to ambiguities of expression and obscure figures of speech.[2] Students of American ethnology are familiar with the fact that in nearly all tribes the language of the sacred songs differs materially from that in daily life.

Of the older grammarians, Father Carochi alone has left us actual specimens of the ancient poetic dialect, and his observations are regretably brief. They occur

---

[1] Clavigero, *Storia Antica di Messico*, Lib. VII, p. 175.

[2] " Ihre Sprachen sind überreich an doppelsinnigen Ausdrücken die sie absichtlich anwenden um ihre Gedanken zu verbergen. Geistliche haben mir versichert, dass sie obgleich der Aztekischen Sprache vollständig mächtig, oft den wahren Sinn einer Beichte nicht zu verstehen vermochten, weil die Beichtende sich in räthselhafter und metaphorreicher Weise auszudrücken pflegten." Carlos von Gagern, *Charakteristik der Indianischen Bevölkerung Mexico's*, p. 17 (in the *Mit. der Geog. Gesell.*, Wien. 1837).

in his chapter on the composition of nouns and read as follows : [1] —

"The ancient Indians were chary in forming compounds of more than two words, while those of to-day exceed this number, especially if they speak of sacred things; although in their poetic dialect the ancients were also extravagant in this respect, as the following examples show:—

1. Tlāuhquéchōllaztalēhualtò tōnatoc.
2. Ayauhcoçamālōtōnamēyòtimani.
3. Xiuhcóyólizítzîlica in teōcuitlahuēhuētl.
4. Xiuhtlapallàcuilōlāmoxtli manca.
5. Nic chālchiuhcozcameca quenmach tòtóma in nocuic.

1. It is gleaming red like the tlauhquechol bird.
2. And it glows like the rainbow.
3. The silver drum sounds like bells of turquoise.
4. There was a book of annals written and painted in colors.
5. I see my song unfolding in a thousand directions, like a string of precious stones."

---

[1] Carochi's translations are not quite literal. The following notes will explain the compounds :—

1. *Tlauitl*, red ochre, *quecholli*, a bird so called, *aztatl*, a heron, *ehualtia*, reverential of *ehua*, to rise up; hence, "It (or he) shone like a noble red-winged heron rising in flight."

2. *Ayauitl*, mist; *coçamalotl*, rainbow; *tonameyotl*, shining, brightness; *ti*, connective; *mani*, substantive verb. "The brightness of the rain bow is there." There is no conjunction "and"; Father Carochi seems to have carelessly taken *ayauh*, which is the form of *ayauitl* in com-

From the specimens presented in this volume and from the above extracts, I would assign the following peculiarities to the poetic dialect of the Nahuatl :—

I. Extreme frequency and richness of metaphor. Birds, flowers, precious stones and brilliant objects are constantly introduced in a figurative sense, often to the point of obscuring the meaning of the sentence.

II. Words are compounded to a much greater extent than in ordinary prose writing.

III. Both words and grammatical forms unknown to the tongue of daily life occur. These may be archaic, or manufactured capriciously by the poet.

IV. Vowels are inordinately lengthened and syllables reduplicated, either for the purpose of emphasis or of meter.

V. Meaningless interjections are inserted for metrical effect, while others are thrown in and repeated in order to express emotion.

VI. The rhetorical figure known as aposiopesis, where a sentence is left unfinished and in an interjectional con-

---

position, for the conjunction *auh*, and. Each of the lines given is a detached fragment, without connection with the others.

3. *xiuitl*, something blue or green; *coyolli*, bells; *tzitzilicaliztli*, tinkling. "The golden drum's turquoise-bell-tinkling."

4. *xiuhtic*, blue or green; *tlapalli*, red; *cuiloa*, to paint or write; *amoxtli*, book; *manca*, imperf. of *mani*. "There was a book painted in red and green."

5. *chalchiuhuitl*, the jade; *cozcatl*, a jewel; *mecatl*, a string; *totoma*, frequentative of *toma*, to unfold, unwind. "I unwind my song like a string of precious jewels."

dition, in consequence of some emotion of the mind, is not rare and adds to the obscurity of the wording.

§ 8. *The Preservation of the Ancient Songs.*

In a passage already quoted,[1] Sahagun imparts the interesting information that the more important songs were written down by the Nahuas in their books, and from these taught to the youth in the schools. A certain branch of the Mexican hieroglyphic writing was largely phonetic, constructed on that method to which I have applied the adjective *ikonomatic*, and by which it was quite possible to preserve the sound as well as the sense of sentences and verses.[2] Such attention could have been bestowed only on the sacred, royal, or legendary chants, while the compositions of ordinary poets would only be disseminated by oral teaching.

By one or both of these methods there was a large body of poetic chants the property of the Nahuatl-speaking tribes, when they were subjugated by the Europeans. Among the intelligent missionaries who devoted their lives to mastering the language and translating into it the doctrines of Christianity, there were a few who felt sufficient interest in these chants to write some of them down in the original tongue. Conspicuous among these was the laborious Bernardino de Sahagun, whose works are our most valued

---

[1] See above, page 10

[2] *On the Ikonomatic Method of Phonetic Writing, with special reference to American Archæology.* By D. G. Brinton, in Proceedings of the American Philosophical Society, for October, 1886.

sources of information on all that concerns the life of the ancient Nahuas. He collected a number of their sacred hymns, translated them into Spanish, and inserted them into the Appendix to the Second Book of his *History of New Spain;* but this portion of his work was destroyed by order of the Inquisition, as a note in the original MS. expressly states.[1]

A certain number, however, were preserved in the original tongue, and, as already noted, we find the able grammarian Horatio Carochi, who published his Grammar of the Nahuatl in 1645, quoting lines from some as furnishing examples of the genuine ancient forms of word-building. He could not, therefore, have doubted their antiquity and authenticity.

A number of these must have come to the knowledge and were probably in the possession of the eminent mathematician and antiquary Don Carlos de Siguenza y Gongora, who lived in the latter half of the same century (died 1700). It was avowedly upon the information which he thought he gleaned from these ancient chants that he constructed his historical theory of the missionary labors of St. Thomas in Mexico in the first century of our era. The title of the work he wrote upon this notion was as follows :—

" Fenix del Occidente San Thomas Apóstol, hallado con el nombre de Quetzalcoatl entre las cenizas de antiguas tradiciones, conservadas en piedras, en Teoamoxtles Tultecas, y en cantares Teochichimecas y Mexicanos."

For many years this curious work, which was never printed

---

[1] This fact is mentioned by Lord Kingsborough in his great work on Mexico, Vol. VI, p. 533.

was supposed to be lost ; but the original MS. is extant, in the possession of the distinguished antiquary Don Alfredo Chavero, of the City of Mexico.[1] Unfortunately, however, the author did not insert in his work any song in the native language nor a literal translation of any, as I am informed by Señor Chavero, who has kindly examined the work carefully at my request, with this inquiry in view.

Half a century later, when Boturini was collecting his material, he found but very few of the old poems. In the catalogue of his MSS. he mentions (XIX, 1) some fragments of ancient songs, badly written, on European paper, but he does not say whether in the original or translated. The same doubt might rest on the two songs of Neza-hualcoyotl named in his Catalogue (V, 2). He does not specifically state that they are in the original. The song of Moquihuix, King of Tlatilulco, in which he celebrated his victory over the Cuextla, which Boturini states in his text (p. 91) as in his possession, is not mentioned at all in his Catalogue, and it is uncertain whether his copy was in Nahuatl.

His literary friend, however, Don Mariano Echevarria y Veitia, removes the uncertainty about the two songs of Nezahualcoyotl, as he informs us that they were in the original tongue, and adds that he had inserted them in his History without translation.[2] I have examined the man-

---

[1] It is described in the *Anales del Museo Nacional*, Tom. III, p. 262.

[2] Echevarria's words are " los pongo en su idioma." *Hist. del Origen de las Gentes que poblaron la Nueva España, Discurso Preliminar, in* Kingsborough's *Mexico*, Vol. VIII.

uscript of his work, now in the Lenox Library, New York City, but it does not contain these texts, and evidently the copy used by Bustamente did not.[1]

Boturini included the translations of the two odes of Nezahualcoyotl in a work on the Virgin of Guadelupe, only a fragment of which has been preserved. One of the chapters in this Latin Essay is entitled *De Indorum Poetarum Canticis sive Prosodiis*, in which he introduces Ixtlilxochitl's translation and also a song in the original Nahuatl, but the latter is doubtless of late date and unimportant as a really native production.[2]

The fragments of Boturini's library collected by M. Aubin, of Paris, contain a number of the original ancient songs of the highest importance, which make us regret the more that this collection has been up to the present inaccessible to students. In his description of these relics published in 1851, M. Aubin refers to the *Historical Annals of the Mexican Nation* (§ VIII, 10, of Boturini's Catalogue) as containing " historical songs in a dialect so difficult that I have not been able to translate them entirely," and adds that similar songs are preserved in others of the ancient annals in his hands.[3]

---

[1] See his *Tezcuco en los Ultimos Tiempos de sus Antiguos Reyes*. Parte IV (Mexico, 1826).

[2] See the description of this fragment of Boturini by Señor Alfreao Chavero in the *Anales del Museo Nacional*, Tom. III, p. 242.

[3] M. Aubin, *Notice sur une Collection d'Antiquités Mexicaines*, pp. 8, 9. (Paris, 1851.)

§ 9. *The LX Songs of the King Nezahualcoyotl.*

The most distinguished figure among the Nahuatl poets was Nezahualcoyotl, ruler of Tezcuco. His death took place in 1472, at the age of eighty years. His father, Ixtlil-xochitl, had been deprived of his possessions and put to death by Tezozomoc, King of the Tepanecas, and until the death of the latter at an advanced age in 1427, Nezahual-coyotl could make but vain efforts to restore the power of his family. Much of the time he was in extreme want, and for this reason, and for his savage persistence in the struggle, he acquired the name "the fasting or hungry wolf"— *nezahual-coyotl.* Another of his names was *Acolmiztli,* usually translated "arm of the lion," from *aculli,* shoulder, and *miztli,* lion.

A third was *Yoyontzin,* which is equivalent to *cevetor nobilis,* from *yoyoma* (*cevere,* i. e., *femora movere in re venerea*) ; it is to be understood figuratively as indicating the height of the masculine forces.

When his power became assured, he proved himself a liberal and enlightened patron of the arts and industries. The poetry and music of his native land attracted him the more as he felt· within himself the moving god, firing his imagination with poetic vision, the *Deus in nobis, calescimus, agitant' illo.* Not only did he diligently seek out and royally entertain skilled bards, but he himself had the credit of composing sixty chants, and it appears that after the Conquest there were that many written down in Roman characters and attributed to him. We need not inquire too closely whether they were strictly his own composition. Perhaps they were framed on themes which he furnished, or were selected by him from those sung at his court by various bards. The history of the works by royal authors everywhere must not be too minutely scanned if we wish to leave them their reputation for originality.

He was of a philosophic as well as a poetic temperament, and reflected deeply on the problems of life and nature. Following the inherent tendency of the enlightened intellect to seek unity in diversity, the One in the Many, he reached the conclusion to which so many thinkers in all ages and of all races have been driven, that underlying all phenomena is one primal and adequate Cause, the Essence of all Existence. This conclusion he expressed in a philosophic apothegm which was preserved by his disciples, in these words :—

Ipan in chicunauitlamanpan meztica in tloque nahuaque palne nohuani teyocoyani icel teotl oquiyocox in ixquex quexquex in ittoni ihuan amo ittoni.

"In the ninth series is the Cause of All, of us and of all created things, the one only God who created all things both visible and invisible."[1]

To perpetuate the memory of this philosophic deduction he caused to be constructed at Tezcuco a stone tower nine stories in height, the ruins of which were visible long after the Spanish occupation. To this tower he gave the name Chililitli, a term of uncertain meaning, but which we find was applied in Tenochtitlan to a building- sacred

---

[1] Printed very incorrectly in Lord Kingsborough's edition of Ixtlilxochitl's *Relaciones Historicas* (Rel. X, Kingsborough, *Antiquities of Mexico*, Vol. IX, p. 454).

to the Nine Winds.[1] To explain the introduction of this number, I should add that a certain school of Nahuatl priests taught that the heaven above and the earth below were each divided into nine concentric arcs, each leading farther and farther away from the conditions of the present life. Hence, there were nine heavens, abodes of the gods, and nine lower regions, abodes of the souls of the dead. Another school taught that there were not nine but thirteen of these stages.

The sixty poems by Nezahualcoyotl are mentioned by various writers as in existence after the Conquest, reduced to writing in the original tongue, and of several of them we have translations or abstracts.[2] Of four the translations claim to be complete, and were published entire for the first time in the original Spanish by Lord Kingsborough in the ninth volume of his great work on the *Antiquities of Mexico*. Since then they have received various renderings in prose and verse into different languages at the hands of modern writers.

I shall give a literal prose translation from the Spanish, numbering the poems and their verses, for convenience of reference, in the order in which they appear in the pages of Lord Kingsborough.

---

[1] See Sahagun, *Historia de Nueva España*, Lib. II, Appendix.

[2] Bustamente puts the number of the songs of Nezahualcoyotl at eighty, of which he could find only one extant, and this, as I understand his words, in Spanish only. See his *Tezcuco en los Tiempos de sus Antiguous Reyes*, p. 253 (Mexico, 1826). When Alexander von Humboldt visited Mexico he sought in vain for any fragment of the songs of the royal bard. *Vues des Cordillères*, etc., Tom. II, p. 391.

The first is one referred to, and partly translated by Ixtlilxochitl, in his *Historia Chichimeca* (cap. 47). He calls it a *xopancuicatl* (see ante, p. 15), and states that it was composed and sung on the occasion of the banquet when the king laid the foundations of his great palace. He gives the first words in the original as follows:—

Tlaxoconcaguican ani Nezahualcoyotzin;

And the translation:—

" Hear that which says the King Nezahualcoyotl."

Restoring the much mutilated original to what I should think was its proper form, the translation should read:—

"Listen attentively to what I, the singer, the noble Nezahualcoyotl, say:"—

I.

1. Listen with attention to the lamentations which I, the King Nezahualcoyotl, make upon my power, speaking with myself, and offering an example to others.

2. O restless and striving king, when the time of thy death shall come, thy subjects shall be destroyed and driven forth; they shall sink into dark oblivion. Then in thy hand shall no longer be the power and the rule, but with the Creator, the All-powerful.

3. He who saw the palaces and court of the old King Tezozomoc, how flourishing and powerful was his sway, may see them now dry and withered; it seemed as if they should last forever, but all that the world offers is illusion and deception, as everything must end and die.

4. Sad and strange it is to see and reflect on the pros-

perity and power of the old and dying King Tezozomoc;
watered with ambition and avarice, he grew like a willow
tree rising above the grass and flowers of spring, rejoicing
for a long time, until at length, withered and decayed,
the storm wind of death tore him from his roots, and
dashed him in fragments to the ground. The same fate
befell the ancient King Colzatzli, so that no memory was
left of him, nor of his lineage.

5. In these lamentations and in this sad song, I now
call to memory and offer as an example that which takes
place in the spring, and the end which overtook King
Tezozomoc; and who, seeing this, can refrain from tears
and wailing, that these various flowers and rich delights
are bouquets that pass from hand to hand and all wither
and end even in the present life!

6. Ye sons of kings and mighty lords, ponder well and
think upon that which I tell you in these my lamentations, of what takes place in spring and of the end which
overtook King Tezozomoc; and who, seeing this, can
refrain from tears and wailing that these various flowers
and rich delights are bouquets that pass from hand to hand
and all wither and end even in the present life!

7. Let the birds now enjoy, with melodious voices, the
abundance of the house of the flowery spring, and the
butterflies sip the nectar of its flowers.

The second song is preserved in a Spanish metrical
translation only, but which from internal evidence I should
judge to be quite literal. The words of the poem do not

represent it as a composition by the royal poet, but one which was sung before him, and addressed to him. It admonishes him to rejoice in the present moment, as the uncertainties of life and fate must at some time, perhaps very soon, deprive him of their enjoyment.

II.

1. I wish to sing for a moment, since time and occasion are propitious; I hope to be permitted, as my intention merits it, and I begin my song, though it were better called a lamentation.

2. And thou, beloved companion, enjoy the beauty of these flowers, rejoice with me, cast out fears, for if pleasure ends with life, so also does pain.

3. I, singing, will touch the sonorous instrument, and thou, rejoicing in the flowers, dance and give pleasure to God the powerful. Let us be happy in the present, for life is transitory.

4. Thou hast placed thy noble court in Acolhuacan, thine are its lintels, thou hast decked them, and one may well believe that with such grandeur thy state shall increase and grow.

5. O prudent Yoyontzin, famous king and peerless monarch, rejoice in the present, be happy in the springtime, for a day shall come in which thou shalt vainly seek these joys.

6. Then thy destiny shall snatch the sceptre from thy hand, thy moon shall wane, no longer wilt thou be strong and proud, then thy servants shall be destitute of all things.

7. In this sad event, the nobles of thy line, the provinces of might, children of noble parents, lacking thee as their lord, shall taste the bitterness of poverty.

8. They shall call to mind how great was thy pomp, thy triumphs and victories, and bewailing the glory and majesty of the past, their tears will flow like seas.

9. These thy descendants who serve thy plume and crown, when thou art gone, will forsake Culhuacan, and as exiles will increase their woes.

10. Little will fame have to tell of this wondrous majesty, worthy of a thousand heralds; the nations will only remember how wisely governed the three chieftains who held the power,

11. At Mexico, Montezuma the famous and valorous, at Culhuacan the fortunate Nezahualcoyotl, and at the stronghold of Acatlapan, Totoquilhuatli.

12. I fear no oblivion for thy just deeds, standing . as thou dost in thy place appointed by the Supreme Lord of All, who governs all things.

13. Therefore, O Nezahualcoyotl, rejoice in what the present offers, crown thyself with flowers from thy gardens, hear my song and music which aim to please thee.

14. The pleasures and riches of this life are but loaned, their substance is vain, their appearance illusory; and so true is this that I ask thee for an answer to these questions :

15. What has become of Cihuapan? Of the brave Quantzintecomatzin ? Of Conahuatzin ? What of all these people ? Perhaps these very words have already passed into another life.

16. Would that we who are now united by the ties of

D

love and friendship could foresee the sharp edge of death, for nothing is certain, and the future ever brings changes.

The third is a "spring song" in which the distinguished warriors of the king are compared to precious stones. Such jewels were believed by the Nahuas to possess certain mysterious powers as charms and amulets, a belief, it is needless to say, found among almost all nations. In verse 18 there is a reference to the superstition that at dawn, when these jewels are exposed to the first rays of the sun, they emit a fine vapor which wafts abroad their subtle potency. The poem is in Spanish verse, and the original is said to have been written down by Don Fernando de Avila, governor of Tlalmanalco, from the mouth of Don Juan de Aguilar, governor of Cultepec, a direct descendant of Nezahualcoyotl.

III.

1. The flowery spring has its house, its court, its palace, adorned with riches, with goods in abundance.

2. With discreet art they are arranged and placed, rich feathers, precious stones, surpassing in luster the sun.

3. There is the valued carbuncle, which from its beauteous center darts forth rays which are the lights of knowledge.

4. There is the prized diamond, sign of strength, shooting forth its brilliant gleams.

5. Here one sees the translucent emerald suggesting the hope of the rewards of merit.

6. Next follows the topaz, equaling the emerald, for the reward it promises is a heavenly dwelling.

7. The amethyst, signifying the cares which a king has for his subjects, and moderation in desires.

8. These are what kings, princes and monarchs delight to place upon their breasts and crowns.

9. All these stones with their varied and singular virtues, adorn Thy house and court, O Father, O Infinite God!

10. These stones which I the King Nezahualcoyotl have succeeded in uniting in loving liens,

11. Are the famous princes, the one called Axaxacatzin, the other Chimalpopoca, and Xicomatzintlamata.

12. To-day, somewhat rejoiced by the joy and words of these, and of the other lords who were with them,

13. I feel, when alone, that my soul is pleased but for a brief time, and that all pleasure soon passes.

14. The presence of these daring eagles pleases me, of these lions and tigers who affright the world,

15. These who by their valor win everlasting renown, whose name and whose deeds fame will perpetuate.

16. Only to-day am I glad and look upon these rich and varied stones, the glory of my bloody battles.

17. To-day, noble princes, protectors of the realm, my will is to entertain you and to praise you.

18. It seems to me that ye answer from your souls, like the fine vapor arising from precious stones,—

19. "O King Nezahualcoyotl, O royal Montezuma, your subjects sustain themselves with your soft dews.

20. "But at last a day shall come which will cut away this power, and all these will be left wretched orphans.

21. "Rejoice, mighty King, in this lofty power which the King of Heaven has granted you, rejoice and be glad.

22. "In the life of this world there is no beginning anew, therefore rejoice, for all good ends.

23. "The future promises endless changes, griefs that your subjects will have to undergo.

24. "Ye see before you the instruments decked with wreaths of odorous flowers; rejoice in their fragrance.

25. "To-day there are peace, and goodfellowship; therefore let all join hands and rejoice in the dances,

26. "So that for a little while princes and kings and the nobles may have pleasure in these precious stones,

27. "Which through his goodness the will of the King Nezahualcoyotl has set forth for you, inviting you to-day to his house."

The fourth song has been preserved in an Otomi translation by the Mexican antiquary Granados y Galvez,[1] and in an abstract by Torquemada.[2] The latter gives the first words as follows:—

Xochitl mamani in huehuetitlan:

Which he translates:—

"There are fresh and fragrant flowers among the groves."

---

[1] *Tardes Americanas*, pp. 90–94. (Mexico, 1778.)

[2] Torquemada, *Monarquia Indiana*, Lib. II, cap. 45. The word *huehuetitlan*, seems to be a misprint for *ahuehuetitlan*, from *ahuehuetl*, with the ligature *ti*, and the postposition *tlan*, literally " among the cypresses."

It is said to have been composed at the time the king dedicated his palace.

IV.

1. The fleeting pomps of the world are like the green willow trees, which, aspiring to permanence, are consumed by a fire, fall before the axe, are upturned by the wind, or are scarred and saddened by age.

2. The grandeurs of life are like the flowers in color and in fate ; the beauty of these remains so long as their chaste buds gather and store the rich pearls of the dawn and saving it, drop it in liquid dew ; but scarcely has the Cause of All directed upon them the full rays of the sun, when their beauty and glory fail, and the brilliant gay colors which decked forth their pride wither and fade.

3. The delicious realms of flowers count their dynasties by short periods ; those which in the morning revel proudly in beauty and strength, by evening weep for the sad destruction of their thrones, and for the mishaps which drive them to loss, to poverty, to death and to the grave. All things of earth have an end, and in the midst of the most joyous lives, the breath falters, they fall, they sink into the ground.

4. All the earth is a grave, and nought escapes it ; nothing is so perfect that it does not fall and disappear. The rivers, brooks, fountains and waters flow on, and never return to their joyous beginnings ; they hasten on to the vast realms of Tlaloc, and the wider they spread between their marges the more rapidly do they mould their own sepulchral urns. That which was yesterday is

not to-day; and let not that which is to-day trust to live to-morrow.

5. The caverns of earth are filled with pestilential dust which once was the bones, the flesh, the bodies of great ones who sate upon thrones, deciding causes, ruling assemblies, governing armies, conquering provinces, possessing treasures, tearing down temples, flattering themselves with pride, majesty, fortune, praise and dominion. These glories have passed like the dark smoke thrown out by the fires of Popocatepetl, leaving no monuments but the rude skins on which they are written.

6. Ha! ha! Were I to introduce you into the obscure bowels of this temple, and were to ask you which of these bones were those of the powerful Achalchiuhtlanextin, first chief of the ancient Toltecs; of Necaxecmitl, devout worshiper of the gods; if I inquire where is the peerless beauty of the glorious empress Xiuhtzal, where the peaceable Topiltzin, last monarch of the hapless land of Tulan; if I ask you where are the sacred ashes of our first father Xolotl; those of the bounteous Nopal; those of the generous Tlotzin; or even the still warm cinders of my glorious and immortal, though unhappy and luckless father Ixtlilxochitl; if I continued thus questioning about all our august ancestors, what would you reply? The same that I reply—I know not, I know not; for first and last are confounded in the common clay. What was their fate shall be ours, and of all who follow us.

7. Unconquered princes, warlike chieftains, let us seek, let us sigh for the heaven, for there all is eternal, and nothing is corruptible. The darkness of the sepulchre is

but the strengthening couch for the glorious sun, and the obscurity of the night but serves to reveal the brilliancy of the stars. No one has power to alter these heavenly lights, for they serve to display the greatness of their Creator, and as our eyes see them now, so saw them our earliest ancestors, and so shall see them our latest posterity.

It will be seen that the philosophy of these songs is mostly of the Epicurean and *carpe diem* order. The certainty of death and the mutability of fortune, observations which press themselves upon the mind of man everywhere, are their principal staples, and cast over them a hue of melancholy, relieved by exhortations to enjoy to the utmost what the present moment offers of pleasure and sensual gratification. Here and there a gleam of a higher philosophy lights the sombre reflections of the bard; his thoughts turn toward the infinite Creator of this universe, and he dimly apprehends that by making Him the subject of his contemplation, there is boundless consolation even in this mortal life.

Both these leading *motifs* recur over and over again in the songs printed in the original in the present volume, and this similarity is a common token of the authenticity of the book.

§ 10. *The History of the Present Collection.*

The most recent Mexican writers formally deny that any ancient Mexican poetry is now extant. Thus the eminent antiquary, Don Alfredo Chavero, in his elaborate work,

México á través de los Siglos, says, " the truth is, we know no specimens of the ancient poetry, and those, whether manuscript or printed, which claim to be such, date from after the Conquest."[1] In a similar strain the grammarian Diario Julio Caballero, writes: " There has never come into our hands a single poetic composition in this language. It is said that the great King Nezahualcoyotl was a poet and composed various songs ; however that may be, the fact is that we have never seen any such compositions, nor met any person who has seen them."[2]

It is important, therefore, to state the exact provenance of the specimens printed in this volume, many of which I consider to have been composed previous to the Conquest, and written down shortly after the Nahuatl language had been reduced to the Spanish alphabet.

All of them are from a MS. volume in the library of the University of Mexico, entitled *Cantares de los Mexicanos y otros opusculos*, composed of various pieces in different handwritings, which, from their appearance and the character of the letter, were attributed by the eminent antiquary Don José F. Ramirez, to the sixteenth and seventeenth centuries.

The copy I have used is that made by the late Abbé Brasseur (de Bourbourg). It does not appear to be complete, but my efforts to have it collated with the original have not been successful. Another copy was taken by the late well-known Mexican scholar Faustino Chimalpopoca,

---

[1] *Op. cit.* Tom. I, p. 795.

[2] *Grammatica del Idioma Mexicano*, p. 180. (Mexico, 1880.)

which was in the possession of Señor Ramirez and sold at the vendue of his books in 1880. It is No. 511 of the catalogue.

The final decision of the age of the poems must come from a careful scrutiny of the internal evidence, especially the thoughts they contain and the language in which they are expressed. In applying these tests, it should be remembered that a song may be almost wholly ancient, that is, composed anterior to the Conquest, and yet display a few later allusions introduced by the person who preserved it in writing, so as to remove from it the flavor of heathenism. Some probable instances of this kind will be pointed out in the Notes.

The songs are evidently from different sources and of different epochs. There are two notes inserted in the MS. which throw some light on the origin of a few of the poems. The first is in connection with No. XII. In my copy of the MS, the title of this song is written twice, and between the two the following memorandum appears in Spanish :

"Ancient songs of the native Otomis, which they were accustomed to sing at their festivals and marriages, translated into the Mexican language, the play and the spirit of the song and its figures of speech being always retained; as Your Reverence will understand, they displayed considerable style and beauty, better than I can express with my slight talent; and may Your Reverence at your convenience approve and be entertained by them, as a skilled master of the tongue, as Your Reverence is."

From its position and from the titles following, this note appears to apply only to No. XII.

The second note is prefixed to No. XIV, which has no title. It is in Nahuatl, and reads as follows:—

I H S

Nican ompehua in cuicatl motenehua melahuac Huexotzin-cayotl ic moquichitoya in tlatoque Huexotzinca mani me-catca; yexcan inic tlatlamantitica, teuccuicatl ahnoço quauhcuicatl, xochicuicatl, icnocuicatl. Auh inic motzot-zona huehuetl cencamatl mocauhtiuh, auh in occencamatl ipan huetzi yetetl ti; auh in huel ic· ompehua centetl ti; auh inic mocuepa quiniquac iticpa huehuetzi y huehuetl, zan mocemana in maitl; auh quiniquac iyeinepantla oc-ceppa itenco hualcholoa in huehuetl; tel yehuatl itech mottaz, ynima ynaquin cuicani quimati iniuh motzotzona; auh yancuican yenoceppa inin cuicatl ychan D. Diego de Leon, Governador Azcapotzalco; yehuatl oquitzotzon in D. Frco Placido ypan xihuitl 1551, ypan in ezcalilitzin tl Jesu Christo.

This may be freely translated as follows:—

†

"Here begins a song called a plain song of Huexotzinco

as it was recited by the lords of Huexotzinco.   These songs
are divided into three classes, the songs of the nobles or
of the eagles, the flower songs, and the songs of destitution.   (Directions follow for beating the drum in unison
with the voices.)   This song was sung at the house of
Don Diego de Leon, Governor of Azcapotzalco ; he who
beat the drum was Don Francisco Placido ; in the year of
the resurrection of our Lord Jesus Christ 1551.''

This assigns beyond doubt the song in question to the
first half of the sixteenth century, and we may therefore
take its phraseology as a type of the Nahuatl poetry shortly
after the Conquest.   It is also stated to be a native composition, and from its contents, it was clearly composed
by one of the converts to the Christian faith.

ANCIENT
NAHUATL POEMS.

I. *Cuicapeuhcayotl.*

1. Ninoyolnonotza, campa nicuiz yectli, ahuiaca xochitl :—Ac nitlatlaniz ? Manozo yehuatl nictlatlani in quetzal huitzitziltin, in chalchiuh huitzitzicatzin ; manozo ye nictlatlani in zaquan papalotl ; ca yehuantin in ma· chiz, ommati, campa cueponi in yectli ahuiac xochitl, tla nitlahuihuiltequi in nican acxoyatzinitzcanquauhtla, ma- noze nitlahuihuiltequi in tlauhquecholxochiquauhtla ; oncan huihuitolihui ahuach tonameyotoc in oncan mocehcemelquixtia ; azo oncan niquimittaz intla one- chittitique ; nocuexanco nictemaz ic niquintlapaloz in tepilhuan, ic niquimellelquixtiz in teteuctin.

2. Tlacazo nican nemi, ye nicaqui in ixochicuicatzin yuhqui tepetl quinnananquilia ; tlacazo itlan in meyaquet- zalatl, xiuhtotoameyalli, oncan mocuica, momotla, mocuica ; nananquilia in centzontlatolli ; azo quinnanan- quilia in coyototototl, ayacachiçahuacatimani, in nepapan tlazocuicani totome. Oncan quiyectenehua in tlaltic- paque hueltetozcatemique.

3. Nic itoaya, nitlaocoltzatzia ; ma namechellelti y tlazohuane, niman cactimotlalique, niman hualtato in quetzal huitzitziltin. Aquin tictemohua, cuicanitzine ? Niman niquinnanquilia niquimilhuia : Campa catqui in yectli, ahuiac xochitl ic niquimellelquixtiz in amohuam- potzitzinhuan ? Niman onechicacahuatzque ca nican tlatimitzittitili ticuicani azo nelli ic tiquimellelquixtiz in toquichpohuan in teteuctin.

4. Tepeitic tonacatlalpa, xochitlalpa nechcalaquiqueo oncan on ahuachtotonameyotimani, oncan niquittacaya in nepapan tlazoahuiac xochitl, tlazohuelic xochitl

I. *Song at the Beginning.*

1. I am wondering where I may gather some pretty, sweet flowers. Whom shall I ask? Suppose that I ask the brilliant humming-bird, the emerald trembler; suppose that I ask the yellow butterfly; they will tell me, they know, where bloom the pretty, sweet flowers, whether I may gather them here in the laurel woods where dwell the tzinitzcan birds, or whether I may gather them in the flowery forests where the tlauquechol lives. There they may be plucked sparkling with dew, there they come forth in perfection. Perhaps there I shall see them if they have appeared; I shall place them in the folds of my garment, and with them I shall greet the children, I shall make glad the nobles.

2. Truly as I walk along I hear the rocks as it were replying to the sweet songs of the flowers; truly the glittering, chattering water answers, the bird-green fountain, there it sings, it dashes forth, it sings again; the mocking bird answers; perhaps the coyol bird answers, and many sweet singing birds scatter their songs around like music. They bless the earth pouring out their sweet voices.

3. I said, I cried aloud, may I not cause you pain ye beloved ones, who are seated to listen; may the brilliant humming-birds come soon. Whom do we seek, O noble poet? I ask, I say: Where are the pretty, fragrant flowers with which I may make glad you my noble compeers? Soon they will sing to me, "Here we will make thee to see, thou singer, truly wherewith thou shalt make glad the nobles, thy companions."

4. They led me within a valley to a fertile spot, a flowery spot, where the dew spread out in glittering splendor, where I saw various lovely fragrant flowers,

ahuach quequentoc, ayauhcozamalotonameyotimani, oncan nechilhuia, xixochitetequi, in catlehuatl toconnequiz,
ma mellelquiza in ticuicani, tiquinmacataciz in tocnihuan
in teteuctin in quellelquixtizque in tlalticpaque.

5. Auh nicnocuecuexantia in nepapan ahuiacxochitl,
in huel teyolquima, in huel tetlamachti, nic itoaya
manozo aca tohuanti hual calaquini, ma cenca miec in
ticmamani; auh ca tel ye onimatico nitlanonotztahciz
imixpan in tocnihuan nican mochipa tiqualtetequizque
in tlazo nepapan ahuiac xochitl ihuan ticuiquihui in
nepapan yectliyancuicatl ic tiquimellelquixtizque in
tocnihuan in tlalticpactlaca in tepilhuan quauhtliya
ocelotl.

6. Ca moch nicuitoya in nicuicani ic niquimicpac
xochiti in tepilhuan inic niquimapan in can in mac
niquinten; niman niquehuaya yectli yacuicatl ic
netimalolo in tepilhuan ixpan in tloque in nahuaque, auh
in atley y maceuallo.

7. Can quicuiz? Can quitlaz in huelic xochitl? Auh
cuix nohuan aciz aya in xochitlalpan, in tonacatlalpan, in
atley y macehuallo in nentlamati? Intla y tlacohua in
tlalticpac ca çan quitemacehualtica in tloque in nahuaque,
in tlalticpac; ye nican ic chocan noyollo noconilnami-
quia in ompa onitlachiato y xochitlalpana nicuicani.

8. Auh nic itoaya tlacazo amo qualcan in tlalticpac ye
nican, tlacazo occecni in huilohuayan, in oncan ca in
netlamachtilli; tlezannen in tlalticpac? tlacazo occecni
yoliliz ximoayan, ma ompa niauh, ma ompa inhuan
noncuicati in nepapan tlazototome, ma ompa nicnotla-
machti yectliya xochitl ahuiaca xochitl, in teyolquima,
in zan tepacca, teahuiaca yhuintia, in zan tepacca, ahuiaca
yhuintia.

lovely odorous flowers, clothed with the dew, scattered around in rainbow glory, there they said to me, " Pluck the flowers, whichever thou wishest, mayest thou the singer be glad, and give them to thy friends, to the nobles, that they may rejoice on the earth."

5. So I gathered in the folds of my garment the various fragrant flowers, delicate scented, delicious, and I said, may some of our people enter here, may very many of us be here; and I thought I should go forth to announce to our friends that here all of us should rejoice in the different lovely, odorous flowers, and that we should cull the various sweet songs with which we might rejoice our friends here on earth, and the nobles in their grandeur and dignity.

6. So I the singer gathered all the flowers to place them upon the nobles, to clothe them and put them in their hands ; and soon I lifted my voice in a worthy song glorifying the nobles before the face of the Cause of All, where there is no servitude.

7. Where shall one pluck them ? Where gather the sweet flowers ? And how shall I attain that flowery land, that fertile land, where there is no servitude, nor affliction ? If one purchases it here on earth, it is only through submission to the Cause of All ; here on earth grief fills my soul as I recall where I the singer saw the flowery spot.

8. And I said, truly there is no good spot here on earth, truly in some other bourne there is gladness ; For what good is this earth ? Truly there is another life in the hereafter. There may I go, there the sweet birds sing, there may I learn to know those good flowers, those sweet flowers, those delicious ones, which alone pleasurably, sweetly intoxicate, which alone pleasurably, sweetly intoxicate.

E

II. *Xopancuicatl, otoncuicatl, tlamelauhcayotl.*

1. Onihualcalac nicuicani nepapan xochitlalpan, huel teellelquixtican, tetlamachtican, oncan ahuach tonam-eyoquiauhtimani, oncan cuicuica in nepapan tlazototome, on cuicatlaza in coyoltototl cahuantimani inin tozquitzin in quellelquixtia in tloque in nahuaque yehuan Dios, ohuaya, ohuaya.

2. Oncan nicaqui in cuicanelhuayotl in nicuicani, tlacazo amo tlalticpac in peuh yectli yancuicatl, tlacazo ompa in ilhuicatl itic hual caquizti in conehua in tlazocoyoltototl in quimehuilia in nepapan teoquecholme zacuantototl, oncan tlacazo quiyectenehua in tloque in nahuaque, ohuaya, ohuaya.

3. Niyolpoxahua in nicaquia ni cuicani, acoquiza in notlalnamiquilizo quin pepetlatiquiza in ilhuicame, nel-cicihuiliz ehecayotiuh in iquinalquixtia in ompa ontlatenehua in zacuanhuitzitzil in ilhuicatl itic, ohuaya, ohuaya.

4. Auh nohuiampa nictlachialtia in noyollo auh tlacazo nelli in amo ixquich quehua in tlazotototl, tlacazo ye oc tlapanahuia in ilhuicatl itic y yollo in tloque in nahuaque mochiuhtica, ca intlacamo teuhyotiuh in notlalnamiquiliz azo huelquinalquixtica ittazo in tlamahuizolli in ilhuicac ic papaqui in ilhuicac tlazototome ixpan in tloque nahuaque, ohuaya, ohuaya.

5. Quenin ah nichocaz in tlalticpac ? ye nican tlacaço onca nemoayá ninoztlacahuia, nicitoa aço zan ye ixquich in nican in tlalticpac ontlamian toyolia, macuele ehuatl in tloque in nahuaque, ma ompa inhuan nimitznocuicatili in ilhuicac mochanecahuan ca noyollo ehua ompa nontlac-hia in monahuac in motloc tipalnemohua, ohuaya, ohuaya.

II. *A Spring Song, an Otomi Song, a Plain Song.*

1. I, the singer, have entered many flower gardens, places of pleasaunce, favored spots, where the dew spread out its glittering surface, where sang various lovely birds, where the coyol birds let fall their song, and spreading far around, their voices rejoiced the Cause of All, He who is God, ohuaya! ohuaya!

2. It is there that I the singer hear the very essence of song; certainly not on earth has true poesy its birth; certainly it is within the heavens that one hears the lovely coyol bird lift its voice, that the various quechol and zacuan birds speak together, there they certainly praise the Cause of All, ohuaya! ohuaya!

3. I, the singer, labor in spirit with what I heard, that it may lift up my memory, that it may go forth to those shining heavens, that my sighs may be borne on the wind and be permitted to enter where the yellow humming bird chants its praises in the heavens, ohuaya! ohuaya!

4. And as in my thoughts I gaze around, truly no such sweet bird lifts its voice, truly the things made for the heavens by the Cause of All surpass all others, and unless my memory tends to things divine scarcely will it be possible to penetrate these and witness the wondrous sights in heaven, which rejoice the sweet heavenly birds before the face of the Cause of All.

5. How much, alas, shall I weep on earth? Truly I have lived here in vain illusion; I say that whatever is here on earth must end with our lives. May I be permitted to sing to thee, the Cause of All, there in the heaven, a dweller in thy mansion, there may my soul lift its voice and be seen with Thee and near Thee, Thou by whom we live, ohuaya! ohuaya!

6. Ma xicaquin nocuic in tinocniuh xochihuehuetl inic tzotzonaya ilhuicacuicatl in nicehuaya, ic niquimellel-quixtia in teteucti, xochicueponi in noyollo izqui xochitl nictzetzelohuaya ic malitiuh in no cuicatzin ixpan in tloque in nahuaque, ohuaya, ohuaya.

III. *Occe al mismo tono tlamelauhcayotl.*

1. Xochicalco nihualcalaquia in nicuicani, oncan icac in chalchiuhuehuetl, oncan chialon ipalnemohuani in teteuctin xochitl tzetzeliuhtimani, tolquatectitla, xoya-caltitlan, onahuiaxtimani in xochicopal tlenamactli huel teyolquima, cahuia ca ihuintia in toyollo ixpan in tloque in nahuaque.

2. Ic motomá tocuic xochiahuia ca ihuinti in toyollo? Aoc ticmati inic nepapan xochicuicatl ic ticcecemeltia in tloque nahuaque quen ahtontlaelehuian; tinocniuh ma nohuehuetitlan ximoquetzaya nepapan xochitl ic ximo-panaya chalchiuh ocoxochitl mocpac xicmanaya xicehua-yan yectli yancuicatl ic melelquixtia in tloque in na-huaque.

3. Tleymach tiquilnamiquia can mach in nemian moyollo ic timoyol cecenmanaya ahuicpa tichuica timoyol popoloaya in tlalticpac? Ca mach titlatiuh xihualmocuepaya xiccaquin yectli yancuicatl ximoyol-ciahuaya xochiaticaya onahuiaxtimani oncan nicehuaya in yectli yancuicatl nicuicani ic nicellelquixtia in tloque in nahuaque.

4. Xihuallachian tinocniuh in oncan icayan xochi-huehuetl tonameyo ontotonauhtimani quetzal ecacehuaz-

6. List to my song, thou my friend, and to the flower-decked drum which kept time to the heavenly song which I sang, that I might make glad the nobles, raining down before them the flowery thoughts of my heart as though they were flowers, that my noble song might grow in glory before the face of the Cause of All, ohuaya! ohuaya!

III. *Another Plain Song, to the Same Tune.*

1. I, the singer, entered into the house strewn with flowers, where stood upright the emerald drum, where awaiting the Giver of Life the nobles strewed flowers around, the place where the head is bowed for lustration, the house of corrupt odors, where the burning fragrant incense spreads and penetrates, intoxicating our souls in the presence of the Cause of All.

2. Where shall we obtain the fragrance which intoxicates our souls? We do not yet know the various flower-songs with which we may rejoice the Cause of All, however desirous we are; thou my friend, would that thou bring to my instrument various flowers, that thou shouldst clothe it in brilliant oco flowers, that thou shouldst offer them, and lift thy voice in a new and worthy song to rejoice the Cause of All.

3. Wherefore should we recall while the soul is in life that our souls must be scattered hither and thither, and that wherever we go we are to be destroyed on earth? Rather let us hide it, turn from it, and listen to some worthy new song; delight thy soul with the pervading fragrance of flowers, as I the singer lift my voice in a new song that I may rejoice the Cause of All.

4. Come hither, thou my friend, to where stands the drum, decked with flowers, gleaming with brightness,

ticaya on xopaleuhtimani in oncan ic chialo ic malhuilo
inipetl in icpal in tloque in nahuaque ; xic cahuaya in
mixtecomatla xihualmocuepaya tohuan, xic ehua in
yancuicatl nicuicani ic niquellelquixtia in tloque in tla-
neciz inic moyollo caltitlan.

5. Tleçannen in nicyocoya in nitlaocolcuica inic
niquimilnamiqui in tepilhuan, in tlazomaquiztin, in
tlazoteoxiuhme, in quetzaltotome, in moteyotico, in
motleyotico in tlalticpac? in ocnoma caquizti inin tenyo,
inin cahuanca, campa neltiazque ? Ca zan titlacatico ca
ompa huel tochan in canin ximoayan inocapa in yolihuayan aic tlamian.

green with the outspread plumes of the quetzal bird, where are looked for and cared for the seats near the Cause of All; leave the place of night and clouds, turn hither with us, lift thy voice in the new song I sing so that I may rejoice the Cause of All, as the dawn approaches in the house of thy heart.

5. Of what use is it that I frame my sad songs, that I recall to mind the youths, the beloved children, the precious relatives, the dear friends, famous and celebrated as they were on earth? Who now hears their fame, their deeds? Where can they find them? All of us are but mortal, and our home is there in the Hereafter, where there is life without end.

IV. *Mexica otoncuicatl.*

1. Nicchalchiuhtonameyopetláhuaya, nictzinitzcanihui-
caloaya, niquilnamiquia nelhuayocuicatla, nic zacuan-
huipanaya yectli yancuicatl nicuicani, nicchalchiuhtlazo-
nenelo ic nichualnextia in xochicueponallotl ic nicellelquixtia in tloque in nahuaque.

2. Zacuantlazoihuiticaya tzinitzcan tlauquechol ic
nicyaimatia, nocuicatzin teocuitlatzitzilini nocuic nitoz;
miahuatototl nocuica cahuantimania, nicehuaya xochitzet-
zelolpá ixpan in tloque nahuaque.

3. Qualli cuicanelhuayotlo, teocuitlaquiquizcopa nicehuaya, ilhuicac cuicatlo nictenquixtia, nitoz miahuatototl, chalciuhtonameyotica, niccueponaltia yectli yancui-
catlo, nicehuaya xochitlenamaquilizticaya ic nitlaahuialia
nicuicani ixpan in tloque nahuaque.

4. Teoquecholme nechnananquilia in nicuicani coyoli-
cahuacaya yectli yacuicatlan, cozcapetlaticaya chachal-
chiuhquetzalitztonameyo xopaleuhtimania xopan xochi-
cuiatl onilhuica ahuiaxtimanio, xochiahuachtitlan nihual-
cuicaya nicuicani.

5. Nictlapalimatia nicxoxochineloaya yectli yancui-
catlan cozcapetlaticaya, etc.

6. Nocontimaloaya nocontlamachtiao xochiteyolquima
cuicatlan poyomapoctli ic ye ahuian ye noyollo, nihual-
yolcuecuechahuaya, nicinecuia ahuiaca, xocomiqui in
noyolia, nicinecuia yectliya xochitla netlamachtiloyan,
xochi ye ihuinti noyolia.

IV. *An Otomi Song of the Mexicans.*

1. I, the singer, polished my noble new song like a shining emerald, I arranged it like the voice of the tzinitzcan bird, I called to mind the essence of poetry, I set it in order like the chant of the zacuan bird, I mingled it with the beauty of the emerald, that I might make it appear like a rose bursting its bud, so that I might rejoice the Cause of All.

2. I skillfully arranged my song like the lovely feathers of the zacuan bird, the tzinitzcan and the quechol; I shall speak forth my song like the tinkling of golden bells; my song is that which the miaua bird pours forth around him; I lifted my voice and rained down flowers of speech before the face of the Cause of All.

3. In the true spirit of song I lifted my voice through a trumpet of gold, I let fall from my lips a celestial song, I shall speak notes precious and brilliant as those of the miaua bird, I shall cause to blossom out a noble new song, I lifted my voice like the burning incense of flowers, so that I the singer might cause joy before the face of the Cause of All.

4. The divine quechol bird answers me as I, the singer, sing, like the coyol bird, a noble new song, polished like a jewel, a turquoise, a shining emerald, darting green rays, a flower song of spring, spreading celestial fragrance, fresh with the dews of roses, thus have I the poet sung.

5. I colored with skill, I mingled choice roses in a noble new song, polished like a jewel, etc. (as in v. 4).

6. I was glorified, I was enriched, by the flower-sweet song as by the smoke of the poyomatl, my soul was contented, I trembled in spirit, I inhaled the sweetness, my soul was intoxicated, I inhaled the fragrance of delicious flowers in the place of riches, my soul was drunken with the flowers.

V. *Otro Mexica tlamelauhcacuicayotl.*

1. Zanio in xochitl tonequimilol, zanio in cuicatl ic huehuetzi in tellel in Dios ye mochan.

2. In mach noca ompolihuiz in cohuayotl mach noca in icniuhyotl in ononoya in ye ichan; ye nio Ioyontzin on cuicatillano ye ipalnemohuani.

3. Ma xiuhquechol xochi, zan in tzinitzcan malintoca zan miqui huaqui xochitl zan ic tonmoquimiloa can titlatoani ya ti Nezahualcoyotl.

4. Ma yan moyoliuh quimati in antepilhuan in anquauhtin amo celo ca mochipan titocnihuan, zancuel achic nican timochitonyazque o ye ichano.

5. Ca ye ompolihuiz in moteyo Nopiltzin, ti Tezozomoctli áca cá ye in mocuica? ayc a nihualchocao ca nihualicnotlamatica notia ye ichan.

6. An ca nihuallaocoya onicnotlamati ayo quico, ayoc quemanian, namech aitlaquiuh in tlalticpac y icanontia ye ichan.

V. *Another Plain Song of the Mexicans.*

1. I alone will clothe thee with flowers, mine alone is the song which casts down our grief before God in thy house.

2. True it is that my possessions shall perish, my friendships, their home and their house; thus I, O Yoyontzin, pour forth songs to the Giver of Life.

3. Let the green quechol birds, let the tzinitzcan twine flowers for us, only dying and withered flowers, that we may clothe thee with flowers, thou ruler, thou Nezahualcoyotl.

4. Ye youths and ye braves, skilled in wisdom, may you alone be our friends, while for a moment here we shall enjoy this house.

5. For thy fame shall perish, Nopiltzin, and thou, Tezozomoc, where are thy songs? No more do I cry aloud, but rest tranquil that ye have gone to your homes.

6. Ye whom I bewailed, I know nevermore, never again; I am sad here on earth that ye have gone to your homes.

VI. *Otro chalcayotl, canto de Tetlepan Quetzanit-zin.*

1. Aua nocnihue ninentlamatia zan ninochoquilia in monahuac aya yehuan Dios, quexquich onmitzicnotla-machtia momacehual cemamanahuac ontonitlanililo in ic tontlahuica tontecemilhuitiltia in tlalticpac.

2. Macazo tleon xoconyoyocoya ti noyollo, yehua cuix ic nepohualoyan in oncan nemohua yehua, in atle tlahuelli in antecocolia huel on yecnemiz in tlalticpac.

3. In quimati noyollo nichoca yehua huel eza ye nelli in titicnihuan, huellenelli nemoa in tlalticpac in tonicniuh tlatzihuiz yehuan Dios.

4. Xontlachayan huitztlampayan, iquizayan in tonatiuh, ximoyollehuayan oncan manian teoatl tlachinolli, oncan mocuica in teucyotl in tlatocayotl yectliya xochitl in amo zannen mocuia, in quetzallalpilo niaya macquauhtica, chimaltica neicaloloyan in tlalticpac ic momacehuaya in yectliya xochitl in tiquelehuia in ticnequia in tinocniuh in quitemacehualtia in quitenemactia in tloque in nahuaque.

5. Nentiquelehuia in tictemoaya in tinocniuh yectliya xochitl can ticuiz intlacamo ximicaliya, melchiquiuhticaya, mitonalticaya ticmacehuaya in yectliyaxochitla, yaocho-quiztli ixayoticaya in quitemacehualtica in tloque in na-huaque.

VI. *Another Chalco-song, a Poem of Tetlepan Quetzanitzin.*

1. Alas, my friend, I was afflicted, I cried aloud on thy account to God. How much compassion hast thou for thy servant in this world sent here by thee to be thy subject for the space of a day on this earth!

2. However that may be, mayst thou so dispose my heart, that it may pass through this place of reckoning, without anger, without injury, and live a good life on earth.

3. My heart knows how truly I weep for my friend, how truly as it lives on earth it cries aloud for thee, my friend, to God.

4. Let thy soul awake and turn toward the south, toward the rising of the sun, rouse thy heart that it turn toward the field of battle, there let it win power and fame, the noble flowers which it will not grasp in vain; adorned with a frontlet of quetzal feathers I went forth armed with sword and shield to the battlefield on earth, that I might merit these noble flowers with which we may rejoice as we wish our friends, as the Cause of All may reward and grant to us.

5. Vainly, O friends, do we desire and seek where we may cull those noble flowers unless we fight with bared breasts, with the sweat of the brow, meriting these noble flowers, in bitter and painful war, for which the Cause of All will give reward.

VII. *Otro.*

1. Tleinmach oamaxque on in antocnihuan in an Chiapaneca Otomi, omachamelelacic: in ic oamihuintiqueo
octicatl in oanquique ic oamihuintique, xicualcuican, in
amo ma in anhuehuetztoqueo, ximozcalicano in antocnihuan nipatiazque in tochano, xopantlalpan ye nican, ma
quiza in amihuintiliz, on xitlachiacano ohuican ye anma-
quia, O!

2. Ca yeppa yuhqui in tizaoctli in tlalticpac, quitema-
cao ohuican ic tecalaquiao teoatl tlachinolli quitoao texaxa-
matzao teopopoloao on canin xaxamanio in tlazochalchi-
hiuitl, in teoxihuitl, in maquiztli tlazotetl in tepilhuan in
coninio in xochitizaoctlio cuel can in antocnihuan in toni-
cahuacao.

3. Ma ye ticiti in xochitlalpan in tochan xochitlalticpac-
ilhuicacpaco in huel ic xochiamemeyallotl on ahuiaxti-
mani, teyolquima yoliliz ahuach xochitl in tochan in
Chiappan, oncan timalolo in teucyotl in tlatocayotl in
chimalxochitl oncuepontimani tonacatlalpan.

4. Quemach in amo antlacaquio in antocnihuan to-
huian tohuiano xicahuacano, in tizaoctlio teoatlachino-
loctli; ma ye ticiti in ompa tinectilo in tochan xochiahua-
choctli, zan ic ahuiaca ihuinti in toyollo, tetlamachtio
teyolquimao tixochiachichinatihui netlamachtiloyan in
toquizayan xochitlalpan tonacatlalpan: tlemach oamax-
queo? xichualcaquican in tocuic in tamocnihuan, etc.

VII. *Another*.

1. What have you done, O you our friends, you Chiapanecs and Otomis, why have you grieved, that you were drunken with the wine which you took, that you were drunken? Come hither and sing : do not lie stretched out; arise, O friends, let us go to our houses here in this land of spring ; come forth from your drunkenness, see in what a difficult place you must take it.

2. For formerly it was so on earth that the white wine was taken in difficult places, as on entering the battlefield, or, as it was said, where the stones were broken and destroyed, where were broken into fragments the lovely emeralds, the turquoises, the honored precious stones, the youths, the children ; therefore take the flowery white wine, O friends and brothers.

3. Let us drink it in the flowery land, in our dwelling surrounded by the flowery earth and sky, where the fountains of the flowers send their sweetness abroad ; the delicious breath of the dewy flowers is in our homes in Chiapas ; there nobility and power make them glorious, and the war-flowers bloom over a fertile land.

4. Is it possible, oh friends, that you do not hear us ? Let us go, let us go, let us pour forth the white wine, the wine of battle ; let us drink where the wine sweet as the dew of roses is set forth in our houses, let our souls be intoxicated with its sweetness; enriched, steeped in delight, we shall soak up the water of the flowers in the place of riches, going forth to a land of flowers, a fertile spot. What have you done ? Come hither and listen to our songs, O friends.

VIII. *Otro, Queuh ce tlatohuani in quimilnamiqui in tlatoque.*

1. Tlaocolxochi ixayoticaya ic nichuipana in nocuic nicuicani, niquimilnamiqui in tepilhuan, in teintoque, in tlaçotitoque in campa in ximohuaya, in oteuctico, in otlatocatico in tlallia icpac, in quetzalhuahuaciuhtoque in chalchiuhteintoque in tepilhuan, in maoc imixpan in maoc oquitlani; in ye itto in tlalticpac iximachoca in tloque in nahuaque.

2. Y yo ya hue nitlaocolcuicaya in niquimilnamiqui in tepilhuan, ma zan itla ninocuepa, ma niquimonana, ma niquinhualquixti in ompa in ximoayan, ma oc oppa tihua in tlalticpac, ma oc quimahuizoqui in tepilhuan in ticmahuizoa, azo huel yehuantin tlatlazomahuizozquia in ipalnemohualoni, quemmach tomazehual in tlazaniuh ticmatican in ticnopillahueliloque ic choca in noyollo nino tlalnamiquiliz huipana in nicuicani choquiztica tlaocoltica nitlalnamiquia.

3. Manozo zan nicmati in nechcaquizque intla itla yectli cuicatl niquimehuili in ompa ximohuayan, ma ic niqui-papacti, ma ic niquimacotlaza inin tonez inin chichina-quiliz in tepilhuan. Cuix on machiaz? Quennel nihu-alnellaquahua? Aquen manian ompa niquimontocaz? Ano niquin nonotztaciz in ye yuh quin in tlalticpac.

VIII. *Composed by a Certain Ruler in Memory of Former Rulers.*

1. Weeping, I, the singer, weave my song of flowers of sadness; I call to memory the youths, the shards, the fragments, gone to the land of the dead; once noble and powerful here on earth, the youths were dried up like feathers, were split into fragments like an emerald, before the face and in the sight of those who saw them on earth, and with the knowledge of the Cause of All.

2. Alas! alas! I sing in grief as I recall the children. Would that I could turn back again; would that I could grasp their hands once more; would that I could call them forth from the land of the dead; would that we could bring them again on earth, that they might rejoice and we rejoice, and that they might rejoice and delight the Giver of Life; is it possible that we His servants should reject him or should be ungrateful? Thus I weep in my heart as I, the singer, review my memories, recalling things sad and grievous.

3. Would only that I knew they could hear me, there in the land of the dead, were I to sing some worthy song. Would that I could gladden them, that I could console the suffering and the torment of the children. How can it be learned? Whence can I draw the inspiration? They are not where I may follow them; neither can I reach them with my calling as one here on earth.

F

IX. *Otro Tlaocolcuica Otomitl.*

1. In titloque in tinahuaque nimitzontlaocolnonotzaya,
nelcicihuiliz mixpantzinco noconiyahuaya, ninentlamati
in tlalticpac ye nican nitlatematia, ninotolinia, in ayc
onotechacic in pactli, in necuiltonolli ye nican ; tlezannen
naicoyc amo y mochiuhyan, tlacazo atle nican xotlacueponi in nentlamachtillia, tlacazo zan ihuian in motloc in
monahuac ; Macuelehuatl ma xicmonequilti ma mona-
huactzinco oc ehuiti in noyolia, ninixayohuatzaz in motloc
monahuac tipalnemohuani.

2. Quemachamiqueo in motimalotinemi co y in
tlalticpac in ayac contenmatio in atlamachilizneque o
tlacazo can moztla cahuia on in ămitztenmati in titloque
in tinahuaque inic momatio ca mochipa tlalticpac,
nemizqueo ninotlamatli motlaliao niquimittao, tlacazo
mixitl tlapatl oquiqueo ic nihualnelaquahua in ninotolinia o tlacazo ompa in ximohuayan neittotiuh o, cazo
tiquenamiqueo quiniquac ye pachihuiz ye teyolloa.

3. Ma cayac quen quichihuaya in iyollo in tlalticpac
ye nican in titlaocaxtinemi in tichocatinemia, ca zacuel
achic ontlaniizoo, tlacazo zan tontlatocatihuio in yuho
otlatocatque tepilhuan, ma ic ximixcuiti in tinocniuh in
atonahuia in atihuelamati in tlalticpac o ; ma oc ye
ximăpana in tlaocolxochitl, choquizxochitl, xoyocatimalo
o xochielcicihuiliztlio in ihuicpa toconiyahuazon in tloque
in nahuaque.

4. Ica ye ninapanao tlaocolxochicozcatlon, nomac
ommanian elcicihuilizchimàlxochitlon, nic ehuaya in
tlaocolcuicatloo, nicchalchiuhcocahuicomana yectli yancuicatl, nic ahuachxochilacatzoa, yn o chalchiuhue-
hueuhilhuitl, itech nictlaxilotia in nocuicatzin in nicuicani
ye niquincuilia in ilhuicac chanequeo zacuantototl,
quetzaltzinitzcantototl teoquechol inon tlătoa quechol in
qui cecemeltia in tloque, etc.

IX. *An Otomi Song of Sadness.*

1. To thee, the Cause of All, to thee I cried out in sadness, my sighs rose up before thy face; I am afflicted here on earth, I suffer, I am wretched, never has joy been my lot, never good fortune; my labor has been of no avail, certainly nothing here lessens one's suffering; truly only to be with thee, near thee; may it be thy will that my soul shall rise to thee, may I pour out my tears to thee, before thee, O thou Giver of Life.

2. Happy are those who walk in thy favor here on earth, who never neglect to offer up praise, nor, leaving till to-morrow, neglect thee, thou Cause of All, that thou mayest be known in all the earth; I know that they shall live, I see that they are established, certainly they have drunk to forgetfulness while I am miserable, certainly I shall go to see the land of the dead, certainly we shall meet where all souls are contented.

3. Never were any troubled in spirit on the earth who appealed to thee, who cried to thee, only for an instant were they cast down, truly thou caused them to rule as they ruled before: Take as an example on earth, O friend, the fever-stricken patient; clothe thyself in the flowers of sadness, in the flowers of weeping, give praises in flowers of sighs that may carry you toward the Cause of All.

4. I array myself with the jewels of saddest flowers; in my hands are the weeping flowers of war; I lift my voice in sad songs; I offer a new and worthy song which is beautiful and melodious; I weave songs fresh as the dew of flowers; on my drum decked with precious stones and plumes I, the singer, keep time to my song, as I take it from those dwellers in the heavens, the zacuan bird, the beautiful tzinitzcan, the divine quechol, those melodious birds who give joy to the Cause of All.

X. *Mexica xopancuicatl tlamelauhcayotl.*

1. Tlaocoya in noyollo nicuicanitl nicnotlamatia, yehua za yey xochitl y zan ye in cuicatlin, ica nitlacocoa in tlalticpac ye nican, ma nequitocan intech cocolia intech miquitlani moch ompa onyazque cano y ichan, ohuaya.

2. I inquemanian in otonciahuic, in otontlatzihuic tocon ynayaz in momahuizco in motenyo in tlalticpac, ma nenquitocane, ohuaya, etc.

3. Inin azan oc huelnemohuan in tlalticpac mazano ihuian yehuan Dios quiniquac onnetemoloa in tiaque in canin ye ichan, ohuaya.

4. Hu inin titotolinia ma yuhquitimiquican ma omochiuh in mantech onittocan in tocnihuan in matech onahuacan in quauhtin y a ocelotl.

5. Mazo quiyocoli macaoc xictemachican, can antlahuicaya y caya amechmotlatili in ipalnemohuani, ohuaya.

6. Ay ya yo xicnotlamatican Tezcacoacatl, Atecpanecatl mach nel amihuihuinti in cozcatl in chalchihuitli, ma ye anmonecti, ma ye antlaneltocati.

X. *A Spring Song of the Mexicans, a Plain Song.*

1. My heart grieved, I, the singer, was afflicted, that these are the only flowers, the only songs which I can procure here on earth; see how they speak of sickness and of death, how all go there to their homes, alas.

2. Sometimes thou hast toiled and acquired skill, thou takest refuge in thy fame and renown on earth; but see how vain they speak, alas.

3. As many as live on earth, truly they go to God when they descend to the place where are their homes, alas.

4. Alas, we miserable ones, may it happen when we die that we may see our friends, that we may be with them in grandeur and strength.

5. Although He is the Creator, do not hope that the Giver of Life has sent you and has established you.

6. Be ye grieved, ye of Tezcuco and Atecpan, that ye are intoxicated with gems and precious stones; come forth to the light, come and believe.

XI. *Otro.*

1. Nicchocaehua, nicnotlamati, nicelnamiqui ticauhte-
huazque yectliya xochitl yectli yancuicatl; ma oc tonahui-
acan, ma oc toncuicacan cen tiyahui tipolihui ye ichan,
etc.

2. Achtleon ah yuhquimati in tocnihuan cocoya in
noyollo qualani yehua ay oppan in tlacatihua ye ay oppa
piltihuaye yece yequi xoantlalticpac.

3. Oc achintzinca y tetloc ye nican tenahuacan aic
yezco on aic nahuiaz aic nihuelamatiz.

4. In can on nemian noyollo yehua? Can huel ye no-
chan? Can huel nocallamanian? Ninotolinia tlalticpac.

5. Zan ye tocontemaca ye tocontotoma in mochalchiuh,
ye on quetzalmalintoc, zacuan icpac xochitl, za yan
tiquinmacayan tepilhuan O.

6. In nepapan xochitl conquimilo, conihuiti ye
noyollo niman nichocaya ixpan niauh in tonan.

7. Zan nocolhuia: ipalnemohua ma ca ximozoma,
ma ca ximonenequin tlalticpac, mazo tehuantin motloc
tinemican y, zan ca ye moch ana ilhuicatlitica.

8. Azo tle nello nicyaitohua nican ipalnemohua, zan
tontemiqui y, zan toncochitlehuaco, nicitoa in tlalticpac
ye ayac huel tontiquilhuia ye nicana.

9. In manel ye chalchihuitl, mantlamatilolli, on aya
mazo ya ipalnemohuani ayac hueltic ilhuia nicana.

XI. *Another.*

1. I lift my voice in wailing, I am afflicted, as I remember that we must leave the beautiful flowers, the noble songs; let us enjoy ourselves for a while, let us sing, for we must depart forever, we are to be destroyed in our dwelling place.

2. Is it indeed known to our friends how it pains and angers me that never again can they be born, never again be young on this earth?

3. Yet a little while with them here, then nevermore shall I be with them, nevermore enjoy them, nevermore know them.

4. Where shall my soul dwell? Where is my home? Where shall be my house? I am miserable on earth.

5. We take, we unwind the jewels, the blue flowers are woven over the yellow ones, that we may give them to the children.

6. Let my soul be draped in various flowers; let it be intoxicated by them, for soon must I weeping go before the face of our mother.

7. This only do I ask:—Thou Giver of Life, be not angry, be not severe on earth, let us live with thee on earth, take us to the Heavens.

8. But what can I speak truly here of the Giver of Life? We only dream, we are plunged in sleep; I speak here on earth; but never can we speak in worthy terms here.

9. Although it may be jewels and precious ointments (of speech), yet of the Giver of Life, one can never here speak in worthy terms.

XII. *Xopancuicatl nenonotzalcuicatl ipampa in aquique amo on mixtilia in yaoc.*

1. Nictzotzonan nohuehueuh nicuicatlamatquetl ic niquimonixitia ic niquimitlehua in tocnihuan in atle in yollo quimati in aic tlathui ipan inin yollo yaocochmictoque in inpan motimaloa in mixtecomatlayohualli anen niquito huay motolinia y, maquicaqui qui y xochitlathuicacuicatl occeh tzetzeuhtimania huehuetitlana, ohuaya, ohuai.

2. Tlahuizcalteochitla oncuepontimani in ixochiquiyaopan in tloque in nahuaque, onahuachtotonameyotimani in teyolquima; ma xiqualitacan in atle ipan ontlatao, zannen cuepontimanio ayac mahaca quelehuiao in antocnihuan amo zannen ya xochitl yoliliztlapalneucxochitla e.

3. Quiyolcaihuintiaya in teyolia, zan oncan ye omania, zan oncan ye oncuepontimania quauhtepetitlan in ya hualiuhcancopa y ixtlahuatlitica oncan inemaya oc teoatl tlachinolli a. Oncan in epoyahuayan in teoquauhtli oncan iquiquinacayan, in ocelotl, ipixauhyan in nepapan tlazomaquiztetl, in emomolotzayan in nepapan tlazopilihuitl, oncan teintoque oncan xamantoque in tepilhuan.

4. Tlacuah yehuantin in tepilhuani conelehuiao, in tlahuizcalxochitlan ya nemamallihuao ic tetlanĕnectiao, in ilhuicac onocon iceolitzin yn iotepiltzina quitzetzelotimanio a in tepilhuan in quauhtliya ocelotl, in quimemactiao in xochicueponalotlon in quimihuintia yeyolxochiahuechtlia.

5. In ic timomatia in tinocniuh zan ne yan xochitlon in tiquelehuiaon in tlalticpac, quen toconcuizon quen ticyachihuazon, timotolinia in tiquimiztlacoa a in tepilhuan xochitica cuicatica; ma xihuallachican in atle y ica mitl, ehuaon zan moch yehuantin in tepilhuan zacuanme-

XII. *A Spring Song, a Song of Exhortation, Because Certain Ones did not go to the War.*

1. I strike on my drum, I the skillful singer, that I may arouse, that I may fire our friends, who think of nothing, to whose minds plunged in sleep the dawn has not appeared, over whom are yet spread the dark clouds of night; may I not call in vain and poorly, may they hear this song of the rosy dawn, poured abroad widely by the drum, ohe! ohe!

2. The divine flowers of dawn blossom forth, the war flowers of the Cause of All; glittering with dew they scatter abroad their fragrance; bring them hither that they be not hidden nor bloom in vain, that they may rejoice you our friends, and not in vain shall be the flowers, the living, colored, brilliant flowers.

3. They intoxicate the soul, but they are only found, they blossom only on the lofty mountains, on the broad plains where glorious war finds its home. There is where the eagles gather in bands of sixties, there the tigers roar, there the various beloved stones rain down, there the various dear children are cut to pieces; there the youths are split into shards and ground into fragments.

4. Stoutly do those youths rejoice, laboring for the rose of the dawn that they may win it; and in heaven, He, the only one, the noble one, pours down upon the youths strength and courage, that they may pluck the budding flowers of the pathway, that they may be intoxicated with the dew-damp flowers of the spirit.

5. Know, my friend, that these are the only flowers hich will give thee pleasure on earth; mayest thou take .em and make them; O poor one, search out for thy children these flowers and songs. Look not hither without arrows, let all the youths lift up their voices, like

teoquecholtitzinitzcatlatlauhquecholtin moyeh yectitine-
mio in onmatio in ixtlahuatlitican.

6. Chimalxochitl, quauhpilolxochitl ic oquichtlama-
timani in y antepilhuan xochicozcaocoxochitl ic
mapantimanian, quitimaloao yectliya cuicatl, yectliya
xochitl, imezo imelchiquiuh patiuh mochihuaya in quicelia
on in teoatl tlachinolli; y iantocnihuan tliliuhquitepeca
in tiyaotehua huey otlipana, ma huel xoconmanao y ye
mochimalo, huel xonicaon in ti quauhtliya ocelotla.

XIII. *Huexotzincayotl.*

1. Zan tlaocolxochitl, tlaocolcuicatl on mania Mexico
nican ha in Tlatilolco, in yece ye oncan on neiximachoyan, ohuaya.

2. Ixamayo yectli in zan ca otitech icneli ipalnemohuani, in za can tipopolihuizque in timacehualta, ohuaya.

3. Ototlahueliltic, zan titotolinia timacehualtinquezo
huel tehuantin, otiquittaque in cococ ye machoyan,
ohuaya.

4. Ticmomoyahua, ticxoxocoyan in momacehualy in
Tlatilolco cococ moteca cococ ye machoyan ye ic ticia-
huia ipalnemoani, ohuaya.

5. Choquiztli moteca ixayotl pixahui oncan a in
Tlatilolco; in atlan yahqueon o in Mexica ye cihua
nelihui ica yehuilo a oncan ontihui in tocnihuan a,
ohuaya.

zacuan birds, divine quechols, tzinitzcans, and red quechols, who live joyous lives, and know the fields.

6. O youths, here there are skilled men in the flowers
of shields, in the flowers of the pendant eagle plumes,
the yellow flowers which they grasp; they pour forth
noble songs, noble flowers; they make payment with
their blood, with their bare breasts; they seek the bloody
field of war. And you, O friends, put on your black
paint, for war, for the path of victory; let us lay hands
on our shields, and raise aloft our strength and courage.

XIII. *A Song of Huexôtzinco.*

1. Only sad flowers, sad songs, are here in Mexico, in
Tlatilolco, in this place these alone are known, alas.

2. It is well to know these, if only we may please the
Giver of Life, lest we be destroyed, we his subjects,
alas.

3. We have angered Him, we are only wretched
beings, slaves by blood; we have seen and known affliction, alas.

4. We are disturbed, we are embittered, thy servants
here in Tlatilolco, deprived of food, made acquainted with
affliction, we are fatigued with labor, O Giver of Life,
alas.

5. Weeping is with us, tears fall like rain, here in
Tlatilolco; as the Mexican women go down to the water,
we beg of them for ourselves and our friends, alas.

6. In ic neltic o ya cahua Atloyantepetl o in Mexico
in poctli ehuatoc ayahuitl onmantoc, in tocon ya chihuaya
ipalnemoani, ohuaya.

7. In anMexica ma xiquilnamiquican o yan zan topan
quitemohuia y ellelon i mahuizo yehuan zan yehuan Dios,
yehua anquin ye oncan in coyonacazco, ohuaya.

8. Za can ye oncan zan quinchoquiz tlapaloa o anqui-
huitzmanatl incan yeŭch motelchiuh on ya o anquin ye
mochin, ha in tlayotlaqui, ah in tlacotzin, ah in tlacateuctli in oquichtzin y huihui ica ça ye con yacauhqui in
Tenochtitlan, ohuaya.

9. In antocnihuan ma xachocacan aya ma xăconmati-
can ica ye ticcauhque Mexicayotl huiya, zan ye yatl
chichixhuiya no zan ye tlaqualli chichixaya zan con aya
chiuhqui in ipalnemoani ha in Tlatilolco y, ohuaya.

10. Tel ah zan yhuian huicoque hon in motelchiuhtzin
ha in tlacotzin zan mocuica ellaquauhque ac achinanco
in ahiquac in tlepan quixtiloto in coyohuacan, ohuaya.

6. Even as the smoke, rising, lies in a cloud over Mount Atloyan, in Mexico, so does it happen unto us, O Giver of Life, alas.

7. And you Mexicans, may you remember concerning us when you descend and suffer before the majesty of God, when there you shall howl like wolves.

8. There, there will be only weeping as your greeting when you come, there you will be accursed, all of you, workers in filth, slaves, rulers or warriors, and thus Tenochtitlan will be deserted.

9. Oh friends, do not weep, but know that sometime we shall have left behind us the things of Mexico, and then their water shall be made bitter and their food shall be made bitter, here in Tlatilolco, as never before, by the Giver of Life.

10. The disdained and the slaves shall go forth with song ; but in a little while their oppressors shall be seen in the fire, amid the howling of wolves.

XIV.

1. Zan tzinitzcan impetlatl ipan, ohuaya ; on tzinitzcan
iceliztoca oncan izan in ninentlamatia, in zan icnoxochi-
cuicatica inocon ya temohua ya ohuaya, ohuaya.

2. In canin nemiya icanon in nemitoconchia ye nican
huehuetitlan a ayiahue, ye onnentlamacho, ye mocatlao-
coyalo ay xopancaliteca, ohuaya, ohuaya.

3. Ac ipiltzin ?   Achanca ipiltzin yehuayan Dios Jesu
Christo can quicuilo antlacuiloa quicuilo ancuicatl a
ohuaya, ohuaya.

4. O achan canel ompa huiz canin ilhuicac y xochin-
tlacuilol xochincalitec a ohuaya ohuaya.

5. In ma ontlachialoya in ma ontlătlamahuicolo in
tlapapalcalimanican y ipalnemoa y tlayocol yehuan Dios,
ohuaya.

6. Techtolinian techtlătlanectia y icuicaxochiamilpan,
intechontlătlachialtian ipalnemohua itlayocol yehuan
Dios a ohuaya.

7. Ya ixopantla ixopantlatinenemi ye nican ixtlahuatl
yteey, za xiuhquechol quiahuitl zan topan xaxamacay in
atlixco ya ohuaya, ohuaya.

8. Zan   ye   nauhcampay   ontlapepetlantoc,   oncan
onceliztoc in cozahuizxochitl, oncan nemi in Mexica in
tepilhuan a ohuaya ohuaya.

XIV.

1. Only the tzinitzcan is in power, the tzinitzcan arouses me in my affliction, letting fall its songs like sad flowers.

2. Wherever it wanders, wherever it lives, one awaits it here with the drum, in affliction, in distress, here in the house of spring.

3. Who is the royal son? Is not the royal son, the son of God, Jesus Christ, as was written in your writings, as was written in your songs?

4. Is not the flowery writing within the house of flowers that he shall come there from heaven?

5. Look around and wonder at this scene of many colored houses which God has created and endowed with life.

6. They make us who are miserable to see the light among the flowers and songs of the fertile fields, they cause us to see those things which God has created and endowed with life.

7. They dwell in the place of spring, in the place of spring, here within the broad fields, and only for our sakes does the turquoise-water fall in broken drops on the surface of the lake.

8. Where it gleams forth in fourfold rays, where the fragrant yellow flowers bud, there live the Mexicans, the youths.

XV. *Tezozomoctli ic motecpac.*

1. Zan ca tzihuactitlan, mizquititlan, aiyahue Chico-
moztocpa, mochi ompa yahuitze antlătohuan ye nican,
ohuaya, ohuaya.

2. Nican momalinaco in colcahuahtecpillotl huiya
nican milacatzoa in Colhuaca Chichimecayotl in
toteuchuahuia.

3. Ma oc achitzinca xomotlanecuican antepilhuan
huiya tlacateuhtzin Huitzilihuitl a ya cihuacoatl y
Quauhxilotl huia totomihuacan Tlalnahuacatl aya zan ca
xiuhtototl Ixtlilxochitl y quenman tlatzihuiz quimohmo-
yahuaquiuh yauh y tepeuh yehuan Dios ica ye choca
Tezozomoctli ohuaya ohuaya.

4. Yenoceppa mizquitl yacahuantimani Hueytlalpani,
anquican itlatol yehuan Dios a ohuaya, ohuaya.

5. Can onyeyauh xochitl, can oyeyauh yeh intoca
quauhtli ocelotl huia ya moyahuaya xelihuia Atloyantepetl Hueytlalpan y anquizan itlatol ipalnemohua ohuaya
ohuaya.

6. Oncuiltonoloc, onechtlachtiloc, in teteuctin cemana-
huac y huel zotoca huipantoca y tlătol ipalnemohuani,
huel quimothuitico, huel quiximatico y yollo yehuan
Dios huiya chalchihuitl maquiztliya tlamatelolliya tizatla
ihuitla za xochitl quimatico yaoyotla ohuaya ohuaya.

7. Oya in Tochin y miec acalcatli, Acolmiztlan teuctli
zan Catocih teuctli Yohuallatonoc y yehuan Cuetzpaltzin
Iztaccoyotl totomihuacan Tlaxcallan ohuaye Coatziteuctli Huitlalotzin za xochitl quimatico yaoyotla ohuaya
ohuaya.

XV. *The Reign of Tezozomoctli.*

1. From the land of the tzihuac bushes, from the land of the mezquite bushes, where was ancient Chicomoztoc, thence came all your rulers hither.

2. Here unrolled itself the royal line of Colhuacan, here our nobles of Colhuacan, united with the Chichimecs.

3. Sing for a little while concerning these, O children, the sovereign Huitzilihuitl, the judge Quauhxilotl, of our bold leader Tlalnahuacatl, of the proud bird Ixtlilxochitl, those who went forth, and conquered and ruled before God, and bewail Tezozomoctli.

4. A second time they left the mezquite bushes in Hue Tlalpan, obeying the order of God.

5. They go where are the flowers, where they may gain grandeur and power, dividing asunder they leave the mountain Atloyan and Hue Tlalpan, obeying the order of the Giver of Life.

6. It is cause of rejoicing, that I am enabled to see our rulers from all parts gathering together, arranging in order the words of the Giver of Life, and that their souls are caused to see and to know that God is precious, wonderful, a sweet ointment, and that they are known as flowers of wise counsel in the affairs of war.

7. There were Tochin, with many boats, the noble Acolmiztlan, the noble Catocih, Yohuallatonoc, and Cuetzpaltzin, and Iztaccoyotl, bold leaders from Tlaxcalla, and Coatziteuctli, and Huitlalotzin, famed as flowers on the field of battle.

G

8. Tley an quiyocoya anteteuctin y Huexotzinca? ma
xontlachiacan Acolihuăcan in quatlapanca oncan ye
Huexotla itztapallocan huia yeyahuatimani Atloyantepetl
a ohuaya.

9. Oncan in pochotl ahuehuetl oncan icaca mizquitl ye
oztotlhuiă tetlaquahuac quimatia ipalnemohuani oyao ai
ya hue ohuaya.

10. Tlacateotl nopiltzin Chichimecatl y tleonmach itla
techcocolia Tezozomoctli tech in micitlani ye ehuaya atayahuili quinequia yaoyotl necaliztlon quima Acolhuacan
ohuaya.

11. Tel ca tonehua ticahuiltia ipalnemohuani Colihua
o o Mexicatl y tlahcateotl huiaya atayahuili quinequia
yaoyotl necaliztl qui mana Acolhuacan a ohuaya ohuaya.

12. Zan ye on necuiltonolo in tlalticpac ay oppan
titlano chimalli xochitl ay oppan ahuiltilon ipalnemohua;
ye ic anauia in tlailotlaqui xayacamacha huia ho ay ya
yi ee ohuaya ha ohuaya.

13. Inacon anquelehuia chimalli xochitl y yohual
xochitli tlăchinol xochitl; ye ic neyahpanalo antepilhuan
huiya Quetzalmamatzin Huitznahuacatl ohuaye ho ha
yia yi ee oua yi aha ohuaya.

14. Chimal tenamitl oncan in nemohua yehua necalia
huilotl oyahualla icahuaca yehuaya on canin ye nemi in
tecpipiltin Xiuhtzin xayacamachani amehuano o ancona-
huiltia ipalnemohua ohuaya.

15. In ma huel netotilo mannemamanaloya yaonahuac
a on netlamachtiloyan ipan nechihuallano ohuaye in
tepiltzin can ye mocuetlaca ohuaya, ohuaya.

8. For what purpose do you make your rulers, men of Huexotzinco ? Look at Acolhuacan where the men of Huexotzinco are broken with toil, are trod upon like paving stones, and wander around the mountain Atloyan.

9. There is a ceiba tree, a cypress tree, there stands a mezquite bush, strong as a cavern of stone, known as the Giver of Life.

10. Ruler of men, Nopiltzin, Chicimec, O Tezozomoc-tli, why hast thou made us sick, why brought us to death, through not desiring to offer war and battle to Acol-huacan ?

11. But we lift up our voice and rejoice in the Giver of life; the men of Colhuacan and the Mexican leader have ruined us, through not desiring to offer war and battle to Acolhuacan.

12. The only joy on earth will be again to send the shield-flower, again to rejoice the Giver of Life ; already are discontented the faces of the workers in filth.

13. Therefore you rejoice in the shield-flowers, the flowers of night, the flowers of battle; already are ye clothed, ye children of Quetzalmamatzin and Huitzna-huacatl.

14. Your shield and your wall of safety are where dwells the sweet joy of war, where it comes, and sings and lifts its voice, where dwell the nobles, the precious stones, making known their faces ; thus you give joy to the Giver of Life.

15. Let your dancing, and banqueting be in the battle, there be your place of gain, your scene of action, where the noble youths perish.

16. Quetzalipantica oyo huiloa ahuiltiloni ipalnemohuan yectlahuacan in tapalcayocan a ohuaya ohuaya.

17. Oyo hualehuaya ye tocalipan oyohua yehua Huexotzincatl y tototihua o o Iztaccoyotla ohuaya ohuaya.

18. Ace melle ica tonăcoquiza y nican topantilemonti Tlaxcaltecatl itocoya cacalia in altepetl y Huexochinco ya ohuaya.

19. Cauhtimanizo polihuiz tlalli yan totomihuacan huia cehuiz yiollo o antepilhuan a Huexotzinca y ohuaya ohuaya.

20. Mizquitl y mancan tzihuactli y mancan ahuehuetl onicacahuia ipalnemohua, xonicnotlamati mochi elimanca Huexotzinco ya zanio oncan in huel on mani tlalla ohuaya ohuaya.

21. Zan nohuian tlaxixinia tlamomoyahua y ayoc anmocehuia momăcehual y hualcaco mocuic in icelteotl oc xoconyocoyacan antepilhuan a ohuaya ohuaya.

22. Zan mocuepa itlatol conahuiloa ipalnemohua Tepeyacac ohuaye antepilhuan ohuaya ohuaya.

23. Canel amonyazque xoconmolhuican an Tlaxcalteca y Tlacomihuatzin hui oc oyauh itlachinol ya yehuan Dios a ohuaya.

24. Cozcatl ihuihui quetzal nĕhuihuia oc zo conhuipanque zan Chichimeca y Totomihua a Iztaccoyotl a ohuaya ohuaya.

25. Huexotzinco ya zan quiauhtzinteuctli techcocolia Mexicatl itechcocolia Acolihuiao ach quennelotihua tonyazque quenonamican a ohuaye ohuaye.

16. Dressed in their feathers they go rejoicing the Giver of Life to the excellent place, the place of shards.

17. He lifted up his voice in our houses like a bird, that man of Huexotzinco, Iztaccoyotl.

18. Whoever is aggrieved let him come forth with us against the men of Tlaxcallan, let him follow where the city of Huexotzinco lets drive its arrows.

19. Our leaders will lay waste, they will destroy the land, and your children, O Huexotzincos, will have peace of mind.

20. The mezquite was there, the tzihuac was there, the Giver of Life has set up the cypress; be sad that evil has befallen Huexotzinco, that it stands alone in the land.

21. In all parts there are destruction and desolation, no longer are there protection and safety, nor has the one only God heard the song; therefore speak it again, you children;

22. That the words may be repeated, you children, and give joy to the Giver of Life at Tepeyacan.

23. And since you are going, you Tlaxcallans, call upon Tlacomihuatzin that he may yet go to this divine war.

24. The Chichimecs and the leaders and Iztaccoyotl have with difficulty and vain labor arranged and set in order their jewels and feathers.

25. At Huexotzinco the ruler Quiauhtzin hates the Mexicans, hates the Acolhuacans; when shall we go to mix with them, to meet them?

26. Ay antlayocoya anquimitoa in amotahuan an
teteuctin ayoquantzin ihuan a in tlepetztic in cacha
ohuaya tzihuacpopoca yo huaya.

27. Ca zan catcan Chalco Acolihuaca huia totomihuacan y amilpan in Quauhquecholla quixixinia in ipetl icpal
yehuan Dios ohoaya ohuaya.

28. Tlazoco a ye nican tlalli tepetl yecocoliloya cema-
nahuac a ohuaya.

29. Quennel conchihuazque atl popoca itlacoh in
teuctli tlalli mocuepaya Mictlan onmatia Cacamatl
onteuctli, quennel conchihuazque, ohuaya ohuaya.

XVI.

1. On onellelacic quexquich nic ya ittoa antocnihuan
ayiaue noconnenemititica noyollon tlalticpac y no-
conycuilotica, ay niyuh can tinemi ahuian yeccan, ay
cemellecan in tenahuac y, ah nonnohuicallan in quenon
amican ohuaya.

2. Zan nellin quimati ye noyollo za nelli nicittoa
antocnihuan, ayiahue aquin quitlatlauhtia icelteotl yiollo
itlacoca con aya macan.   Machamo oncan? In tlalticpac
machamo oppan piltihua. Ye nelli nemoa in quenon
amican ilhuicatl y itec icanyio oncan in netlamachtilo y
ohuaya.

3. O yohualli icahuacan teuctlin popoca ahuiltilon
Dios ipalnemohuani : chimalli xochitl in cuecuepontimani
in mahuiztli moteca molinian tlalticpac, ye nican ic
xochimicohuayan in ixtlahuac itec a ohuaya ohuaya.

26. Set to work and speak, you fathers, to your rulers, to your lords, that they may make a blazing fire of the smoking tzihuac wood.

27. The Acolhuacans were at Chalco, the Otomies were in your cornfields at Quauhquechollan, they laid them waste by the permission of God.

28. The fields and hills are ravaged, the whole land has been laid waste.

29. What remedy can they turn to? Water and smoke have spoiled the land of the rulers; they have gone back to Mictlan attaching themselves to the ruler Cacamatl. What remedy can they turn to?

XVI.

1. It is a bitter grief to see so many of you, dear friends not walking with me in spirit on the earth, and written down with me; that no more do I walk in company to the joyful and pleasant spots; that nevermore in union with you do I journey to the same place.

2. Truly I doubt in my heart if I really see you, dear friends; Is there no one who will pray to the one only God that he take this error from your hearts? Is no one there? No one can live a second time on earth. Truly they live there within the heavens, there in a place of delight only.

3. At night rises up the smoke of the warriors, a delight to the Lord the Giver of Life; the shield-flower spreads abroad its leaves, marvelous deeds agitate the earth; here is the place of the fatal flowers of death which cover the fields.

4. Yaonauac ye oncan yaopeuhca in ixtlahuac itec iteuhtlinpopoca ya milacatzoa y momalacachoa yaoxochimiquiztica antepilhuan in anteteuctin zan Chichimeca y ohuaya.

5. Maca mahui noyollo ye oncan ixtlahuatl itic, noconele hua in itzimiquiliztli zan quinequin toyollo yaomiquiztla ohuaya.

6. O anquin ye oncan yaonahuac, noconelehuia in itzi miquiliztli can quinequin toyollo yaomiquiztla ohuaya ohuaya.

7. Mixtli ye ehuatimani yehuaya moxoxopan ipalnemohuani ye oncan celiztimani a in quauhtlin ocelotl, ye oncan cueponio o in tepilhuan huiya in tlachinol, ohuaya ohuaya.

8. In ma oc tonahuican antocnihuan ayiahue, ma oc xonahuiacan antepilhuan in ixtlahuatl itec, y nemoaquihuic zan tictotlanehuia o a in chimalli xochitl in tlachinoll, ohuaya, ohuaya, ohuaya.

4. The battle is there, the beginning of the battle is in the open fields, the smoke of the warriors winds around and curls upward from the slaughter of the flowery war, ye friends and warriors of the Chichimecs.

5. Let not my soul dread that open field; I earnestly desire the beginning of the slaughter, may thy soul long for the murderous strife.

6. O you who are there in the battle, I earnestly desire the beginning of the slaughter, may thy soul long for the murderous strife.

7. The cloud rises upward, rising into the blue sky of the Giver of Life; there blossom forth prowess and daring, there, in the battle field, come the children to maturity.

8. Let us rejoice, dear friends, and may ye rejoice, O children, within the open field, and going forth to it, let us revel amid the shield-flowers of the battle.

XVII. *Xochicuicatl.*

1. Can ti ya nemia ticuicanitl ma ya hualmoquetza xochihuehuetl quetzaltica huiconticac teocuitlaxochinenepaniuhticac y ayamo aye iliamo aye huiy ohuaya, ohuaya.

2. Tiquimonahuiltiz in tepilhuan teteucto in quauhtlo ocelotl ayamo, etc.

3. In tlacăce otemoc aya huehuetitlan ya nemi in cuicanitlhuia zan qui quetzal in tomaya quexexeloa aya icuic ipalnemoa qui ya nanquilia in coyolyantototl oncuicatinemi xochimanamanaya taxocha ohuaya, ohuaya.

4. In canon in noconcaqui in tlatol aya tlacazo yehuatl ipalnemoa quiyananquilia quiyananquilia in coyolyantototl on cuicatinemi xochimanamanaya, etc.

5. In chalchihuitl ohuayee on quetzal pipixauhtimania in amo tlatolhuia, noyuh ye quittoa yayoquan yehuayan cuetzpal ohuaye anquinelin ye quimatin ipalnemoa ohuaya.

6. Noyuh quichihua con teuctlon timaloa yecan quetzalmaquiztla matilolticoya conahuiltia icelteotlhuia achcanon azo a yan ipalnemoa achcanon azo tle nel in tlalticpac ohuaya.

7. Macuelachic aya maoc ixquich cahuitl niquin notlanehui in chalchiuhtini in maquiztini in tepilhuan aya ; zan nicxochimalina in tecpillotl huia : zan ca nican nocuic ica ya nocon ilacatzohua a in huehuetitlan a ohuaya ohuaya.

8. Oc noncoati nican Huexotzinco y nitlătohuani ni teca ehuatzin huiya chalchiuhti zan quetzalitztin y,

XVII. *A Flower Song.*

1. Where thou walkest, O singer, bring forth thy flowery drum, let it stand amid beauteous feathers, let it be placed in the midst of golden flowers;

2. That thou mayest rejoice the youths and the nobles in their grandeur.

3. Wonderful indeed is it how the living song descended upon the drum, how it loosened its feathers and spread abroad the songs of the Giver of Life, and the coyol bird answered, spreading wide its notes, offering up its flowery songs of flowers.

4. Wherever I hear those words, perhaps the Giver of Life is answering, as answers the coyol bird, spreading wide its notes, offering up its flowery song of flowers.

5. It rains down precious stones and beauteous feathers rather than words; it seems to be as one reveling in food, as one who truly knows the Giver of Life.

6. Thus do the nobles glorify themselves with things of beauty, honor and delight, that they may please the one only god, though one knows not the dwelling of the Giver of Life, one knows not whether he is on earth.

7. May I yet for a little while have time to revel in those precious and honorable youths; may I wreathe flowers for their nobility; may I here yet for a while wind the songs around the drum.

8. I am a guest here among the rulers of Huexotzinco; I lift up my voice and sing of precious stones and emer-

niquincenquixtia in tepilhuan aya zan nicxochimalina in
tecpillotl huia ohuaya ohuaya.

9. A in ilhuicac itic ompa yeya huitz in yectliyan
xochitl yectliyan cuicatl y, conpolo antellel conpolo
antotlayocol y in tlacazo yehuatl in Chichimecatl teuctli
in teca yehuatzin ica xonahuiacan a ohuaya ohuaya.

10. Moquetzal izqui xochintzetzeloa in icniuhyotl
aztlacaxtlatlapantica ye onmalinticac in quetzalxiloxo-
chitl imapan onněnemi conchichichintinemi in teteuctin
in tepilhuan.

11. Zan teocuitlacoyoltototl o huel yectli namocuic
huel yectli in anq'ehua anquin ye oncan y xochitl y ya
hualyuhcan y xochitl imapan amoncate in amontlatlătoa
ye ohuaya ohui ohui ilili y yao ayya hue ho ama ha ilili
ohua y yaohuia.

12. O ach ancati quechol in ipalnemoa o ach ancati
tlatocauh yehuan Dios huiya achto tiamehuan anquitzto-
que tlahuizcalli amoncuicatinemi ohui, ohui, ilili, etc.

13. Maciuhtiao o in quinequi noyollo, zan chimalli
xochitl mixochiuh ipalnemoani, quen conchihuaz noyollo
yehua onentacico tonquizaco in tlalticpac a ohuaya
ohuaya.

14. Zan ca yuhqui noyaz in o ompopoliuh xochitla
antlenotleyoye in quemmanian, antlenitacihcayez in
tlalticpac. Manel xochitl manel cuicatl, quen conchihuaz
noyollo yehua onentacico tonquizaco in tlalticpac ohuaya
ohuaya.

15. Manton ahuiacan antocnihuan aya ma on nequech
nahualo nican huiya a xochintlaticpac ontiyanemi yenican
ayac quitlamitehuaz in xochitl in cuicatl in mani a ichan
ipalnemohuani yi ao ailili yi ao aya hue aye ohuaya.

alds; I select from among the youths those for whom I shall wreathe the flowers of nobility.

9. There comes from within the heavens a good flower, a good song, which will destroy your grief, destroy your sorrow; therefore, Chief of the Chichimecs, be glad and rejoice.

10. Here, delightful friendship, turning about with scarlet dyed wings, rains down its flowers, and the warriors and youths, holding in their hands the fragrant xilo flowers, walk about inhaling the sweet odor.

11. The golden coyol bird sings sweetly to you, sweetly lifts its voice like a flower, like sweet flowers in your hand, as you converse and lift your voice in singing, etc.

12. Even like the quechol bird to the Giver of Life, even as the herald of God, you have waited for the dawn, and gone forth singing ohui, etc.

13. Although I wish that the Giver of Life shall give for flowers the shield-flower, how shall I grieve that your efforts have been in vain, that you have gone forth from the world.

14. Even as I shall go forth into the place of decayed flowers, so sometime will it be with your fame and deeds on earth. Although they are flowers, although they are songs, how shall I grieve that your efforts have been in vain, that you have gone forth from the world.

15. Let us be glad, dear friends, let us rejoice while we walk here on this flowery earth; may the end never come of our flowers and songs, but may they continue in the mansion of the Giver of Life.

16. In zancuelachitzincan tlalticpac aya ayaoc noiuhcan quennonamicani cuixocpacohua icniuhtihuay auh in amo zanio nican totiximatizo in tlalticpac y yiao ha ilili yiao.

17. Noconca con cuicatl noconca o quin tlapitzaya xochimecatl ayoquan teuctliya ahuayie, ohuayiao ayio yo ohua.

18. Zan mitzyananquili omitzyananquili xochincalaitec y in aquiauhatzin in tlacateuhtli ayapancatl yahuayia.

19. Can tinemi noteouh ipalnemohuani mitztemohua in quemmanian y mocanitlaocoyan, nicuicanitlhuia, zan ni mitzahuiltiaya ohuiyan tililiyanco huia ohuaya ohuaya.

20. In zan ca izqui xochitl in quetzalizqui xochitl pixahui ye nican xopancalaitec i tlacuilolcalitec, zan nimitzahahuiltiaya ohui.

21. O anqui ye oncan Tlaxcala, ayahue, chalchiuhtetzilacuicatoque in huehuetitlan ohuaye, xochin poyon ayiahue Xicontencatl teuctli in Tizatlacatzin in camaxochitzin cuicatica y melelquiza xochiticaya on chielo itlatol ohuay icelteotl ohuaya.

22. O, anqui nohuia y, ye mochan ipalnemohua xochipetlatl ye noca xochitica on tzauhticac oncan mitztlatlauhtia in tepilhua ohuaya.

23. In nepapan xochiquahuitl onicac, aya, huehuetitlan a a yiahue, can canticaya quetzaltica malintimani, ya, yecxochitl motzetzeloaya ohuaya ohuaya.

24. Can quetzatzal petlacoatl yepac o, ye nemi coyoltototl cuicatinemiya, can quinanquili teuctli ya, conahuiltianquauhtloocelotl ohuaya ohuaya.

16. Yet a little while and your friends must pass from earth. What does friendship offer of enjoyment, when soon we shall no longer be known on earth?

17. This is the burden of my song, of the garland of flowers played on the flute, without equal in the place of the nobles.

18. Within the house of flowers the Lord of the Waters, of the Gate of the Waters, answers thee, has answered thee.

19. Where thou livest, my beloved, the Giver of Life sends down upon thee sometimes things of sadness; but I, the singer, shall make thee glad in the place of difficulty, in the place of cumber.

20. Here are the many flowers, the beauteous flowers, rained down within the house of spring, within its painted house, and I with them shall make thee glad.

21. O, you there in Tlaxcala, you have played like sweet bells upon your drums, even like brilliantly colored flowers. There was Xicontecatl, lord of Tizatlan, the rosy-mouthed, whose songs gave joy like flowers, who listened to the words of the one only God.

22. Thy house, O Giver of Life is in all places; its mats are of flowers, finely spun with flowers, where thy children pray to thee.

23. A rain of various flowers falls where stands the drum, beauteous wreaths entwine it, sweet flowers are poured down around it.

24. Where the brilliant scolopender basks, the coyol bird scatters abroad its songs, answering back the nobles, rejoicing in their prowess and might.

25. Xochitzetzeliuhtoc y, niconnetolilo antocnihuan huehuetitlan ai on chielo can nontlamati toyollo yehua ohuaya ohuaya.

26. In zan ca yehuan Dios tlaxic, ya, caquican yehual temoya o ilhuicatl itic, y, cuicatihuitz, y, quinanquilia o, angelotin ontlapitztihuitzteaya oyiahue yaia o o ohuaya ohuaya.

27. Zan ninentlamatia can niquauhtenco ayahue can * * *

XVIII. *Nican Ompehua Teponazcuicatl.*

Tico, tico, toco, toto, auh ic ontlantiuh cuicatl, tiqui, ti ti, tito, titi.

1. Tollan aya huapalcalli manca, nozan in mamani coatlaquetzalli yaqui yacauhtehuac Nacxitl Topiltzin, onquiquiztica ye choquililo in topilhuan ahuay yeyauh in polihuitiuh nechcan Tlapallan ho ay.

2. Nechcayan Chololan oncan tonquizaya Poyauhte-catitlan, in quiyapanhuiya y Acallan anquiquiztica ye choquililon ye.

3. Nonohualco ye nihuitz ye nihui quecholi nimamali-teuctla, nicnotlamatia oyah quin noteuc ye ihuitimali, nechya icnocauhya nimatlac xochitl, ayao ayao o ayya y yao ay.

4. In tepetl huitomica niyaychocaya, axaliqueuhca nicnotlamatiya o yaquin noteuc (etc. as v. 3).

5. In Tlapallan aya mochieloca monahuatiloca ye cochi-ztla o anca ca zanio ayao, ayao, ayao.

25. Scattering flowers I rejoice you, dear friends, with my drum, awaiting what comes to our minds.

26. It reaches even to God, he hears it seeking him within the heavens, the song comes and the angels answer, playing on their flutes.

27. But I am sad within this wood.   *   *   *

XVIII. *Here begin Songs for the Teponaztli.*

Tico, tico, toco, toto, and as the song approaches the end, tiqui, titi, tito, titi.

1. At Tollan there stood the house of beams, there yet stands the house of plumed serpents left by Nacxitl Topiltzin; going forth weeping, our nobles went to where he was to perish, down there at Tlapallan.

2. We went forth from Cholula by way of Poyauhtecatl, and ye went forth weeping down by the water toward Acallan.

3. I come from Nonohualco as if I carried quechol birds to the place of the nobles; I grieve that my lord has gone, garlanded with feathers; I am wretched like the last flower.

4. With the falling down of mountains I wept, with the lifting up of sands I was wretched, that my lord had gone.

5. At Tlapallan he was waited for, it was commanded that there he should sleep, thus being alone.

H

6. Zan tiyaolinca ye noteuc ic ihuitimali, tinahuatiloya ye Xicalanco o anca zacanco.

7. Ay yanco ay yanco ayamo aya ayhuiya ayanco ayyanco ayamo aye ahuiya que ye mamaniz mocha moquiapana, oquen ye mamaniz moteuccallatic ya icnocauhqui nican Tollan Nonohualco ya y ya y ya o ay.

8. In ye quinti chocaya teuctlon, timalon que ye mămaniz mochan (etc. as v. 7).

9. In tetl, in quahuitl o on timicuilotehuac nachcan Tollan y inon can in otontlatoco Naxitl Topiltzin y aye polihuiz ye motoca ye ic ye chocaz in momacehual ay yo.

10. Zan can xiuhcalliya cohuacallaya in oticmatehuac nachcan Tollan y inon can yn otontlatoco Naxitl Topiltzin (etc. as in v. 9).

6. In our battles my lord was garlanded with feathers; we were commanded to go alone to Xicalanco.

7. Alas! and alas! who will be in thy house to attire thee? Who will be the ruler in thy house, left desolate here in Tollan, in Nonohualco?

8. After he was drunk, the ruler wept; we glorified ourselves to be in thy dwelling.

9. Misfortune and misery were written against us there in Tollan, that our leader Nacxitl Topiltzin was to be destroyed and thy subjects made to weep.

10. We have left the turquoise houses, the serpent houses there in Tollan, where ruled our leader Nacxitl Topiltzin.

XIX.

Tico toco toco ti quiti quiti quiti quito ; can ic mocueptiuh.

1. Tlapapal xochiceutli niyolaya nepapan tonacan
xochitl moyahuaya oncueponti moquetzaco ya naya aya
ye teo ya ixpan tonaa Santa Maria ayyo.

2. An ya ya cuicaya zan quetzala xihuitl tomolihui
yan aya ye nitlachihual icelteotl y ye Dios aya ni itla-
yocolaoya yecoc ya.

3. Zan ca tlaauilolpan nemia moyollo amoxpetlatl
ipan toncuicaya tiquimonyaitotia teteuctin aya in obispo
ya zan ca totatzin aya oncan titlatoa atlitempan ay yo.

4. Yehuan Dios mitzyocox aya xochitla ya mitztlaca-
tilo yancuicatl mitzicuiloa Santa Maria in obispo ya.

XIX.

*Tico, toco, toco, tiquiti, quiti, quiti, quito; where it is to
turn back again.*

1. Resting amid parti-colored flowers I rejoiced; the
many shining flowers came forth, blossomed, burst forth
in honor of our mother Holy Mary.

2. They sang as the beauteous season grew, that I am
but a creature of the one only God, a work of his hands
that he has made.

3. Mayst thy soul walk in the light, mayst thou sing
in the great book, mayst thou join the dance of the rulers
as our father the bishop speaks in the great temple.

4. God created thee, he caused thee to be born in a
flowery place, and this new song to Holy Mary the
bishop wrote for thee.

XX.

1. Tolteca icuilihuia ahaa ya ha on tlantoc amoxtli ya
moyollo ya on aya mochonaciticac o o Toltecayootl aic
aya ninemiz ye nican ay yo.

2. Ac ya nechcuiliz, ac ye nohuan oyaz o, nicaz a anni
icuihuan aya y yancuicanitl y yehetl y noxochiuh non
cuica ihuitequi onteixpan ayyo.

3. Huey in tetl nictequintomahuac quahuitl, nic-
icuiloa yancuicatl itech aya oncan nomitoz in quemmanian in can niyaz nocuica machio nicyacauhtiaz in
tlalticpac, y onnemiz noyol zan ca ye nican ya hualla y
yancoya nolnamicoca nemiz ye noteyo ay yo.

4. Nichocaya niquittoaya nicnotza noyollo ma niquitta
cuicanelhuayotl ayama nicyatlalaquiya ma ya ica tlalticpac quimman mochihua onnenemiz noyol y.   Zan ca
teucxochitl ahuiaca ipotocaticac mocepanoayan toxochiuh ay ye ayao ohuiy on can quiya itzmolini ye nocuic celia notlatollaquillo ohua in toxochiuh icac iqui-
apani ayao.

5. Tel ca cahua xochitl ahuiac xeliuhtihuitz a ipoto-
caya in ahuiyac poyomatlin pixahua oncan ninenenemi
nicuicanitl y ye aya o ohui y on ca quiya itzmolini ye
nocuic celia, etc.

XX.

1. The Toltecs have been taken, alas, the book of their souls has come to an end, alas, everything of the Toltecs has reached its conclusion, no longer do I care to live here.

2. Who will take me? Who will go with me? I am ready to be taken, alas. All that was fresh, the perfume, my flowers, my songs, have gone along with them.

3. Great is my affliction, weighty is my burden; I write out a new song concerning it, that some time I may speak it there where I shall go, a song to be known when I shall leave the earth, that my soul shall live after I have gone from here, that my fame shall live fresh in memory.

4. I cried aloud, I looked about, I reflected how I might see the root of song, that I might plant it here on the earth, and that then it should make my soul to live. The sweet exhalations of the lovely flowers rose up uniting with our flowers; one hears them growing as my song buds forth, filled with my words our flowers stand upright in the waters.

5. But the flowers depart, their sweetness is divided and exhales, the fragrant poyomatl rains down its leaves where I the poet walk in sadness; one hears them growing, etc.

XXI. *Huexotzincayotl.*

Viniendo los de Huexotzinco à pedir socorro à Moteuczoma Tlaxcalla.

1. Tlacuiloltzetzeliuhticac moyoliol tiMoteuczomātzi nichuicatihuitz nictzetzelotihuitz y o huetzcani xochinquetzalpapalotl moquetzalizouhtihuitz noconitotia chalchiuhatlaquiquizcopa niyahueloncuica chalchiuhhuilacapitzli nicteocuitlapitza ya ho ay la ya o haye ohuichile amiyacale.

2. Ohuaya ye onniceelehuia moxochiuh aya ipalnemoani yehuayā Dios aya ilihuāca nahuiche nictzetzeloaya noncuicatilo yaha y.

3. Tozmilini xochitl in noyolyol ay yahue tozmilini xochitl noteponaz ayanco ayancayome oncana y yahue nicxochiamoxtozimmanaya itlatol ayanco ayanca yomeho.

4. Xompaqui xonahuia annochipanicantiyazque ye ichano nohueyetzinteuctli Moteuczomatzi, totlaneuh tlpc totlaneuh uelic xochitl o ayanco.

5. Tlachinoltepec yn ahuicacopa tixochitonameyo timoquetzaco y yehuan Dios a ocelozacatl ypan quauhtli choca ymopopoyauhtoc y yanco y liyan cay yahue ayli y yacalco y ya y yeho zaca y yahue.

6. Ohuaya yehe nipa tlantinemia ixpan Dios a ninozozohuayatlauhquechol, zaquan quetzal in tlayahualol papalotl mopilihuitzetzeloa teixpana xochiatlaquiquizcopa oh tlatoca ye nocuic y yanco ili, etc.

7. Nehcoya ompa ye nihuithuiya xoxouhqui hueyatla ymancan zanniman olini pozoni tetecuica ic nipa tlania,

XXI. *A Song of the Huexotzincos, Coming to Ask Aid of Montezuma Against Tlaxcalla.*

1. Raining down writings for thy mind, O Montezuma, I come hither, I come raining them down, a very jester, a painted butterfly; stringing together pretty objects, I seem to be as one cementing together precious stones, as I chant my song on my emerald flute, as I blow on my golden flute, ya ho, ay la, etc.

2. Yes, I shall cause thy flowers to rejoice the Giver of Life, the God in heaven, as hither I come raining down my songs, ya ho.

3. A sweet voiced flower is my mind, a sweet voiced flower is my drum, and I sing the words of this flowery book.

4. Rejoice and be glad ye who live amid the flowers in the house of my great lord Montezuma, we must finish with this earth, we must finish with the sweet flowers, alas.

5. At the Mount of Battle we bring forth our sweet and glittering flowers before God, plants having the lustre of the tiger, like the cry of the eagle, leaving glorious memory, such are the plants in this house.

6. Alas! in a little while there is an end before God to all living; let me therefore string together beauteous and yellow feathers, and mingling them with the dancing butterflies rain them down before you, scattering the words of my song like water dashed from flowers.

7. I would that I could go there where lies the great blue water surging, and smoking and thundering, till after a time it retires again: I shall sing as the quetzal, the

zan iquetzal in tototl xiuhquechol tototl no chiuhtihuitz'y
ni yahuinac ya Huexotzinco Atzalan ayome.

8. Zan niquintocaz aya niquimiximatitiuh nohueyo-
tzitzinhuan chalchiuhquechol y canca xiuhquechol in
teocuitlapapalotl in cozcatototl ontlapia ye onca Huexotzinco Atzalan ayame;

9. Xochi Atzalaan teocuitlaatl chalchiuhatl y nepa-
niuhyan itlatoaya in quetzalcanauhtli quetzalnocuitlapilli
cuecueyahuaya yliya yliya yaho ayli yaho aye huichile
anicale.

10. Huecapan nicac nicuicanitl huiya zaquan petlatolini,
ma nica yeninemia nicyeyectian cuicatla in nic xochiotia
yayaho yahii.

blue quechol, when I go back to Huexotzinco among the waters (*or*, and Atzalan).

8. I shall follow them, I shall know them, my beloved Huexotzincos; the emerald quechol birds, the green quechol, the golden butterflies, and yellow birds, guard Huexotzinco among the waters (*or*, and Atzalan).

9. Among the flowery waters, the golden waters, the emerald waters, at the junction of the waters which the blue duck rules moving her spangled tail.

10. I the singer stand on high on the yellow rushes; let me go forth with noble songs and laden with flowers.

XXII.

*Tico tico ticoti tico tico ticoti auh ic ontlantiuh in cuicatl
totoco totoco.*

1. Xichocayan nicuicanitl nicitta noxochiuh zan nomac
ommania zan quihuintia ye noyollo ni cuicatl aya nohuian
nemia, zan ca ye noyollo notlayocola in cayo.

2. Xiuhtlamatelolla quetzalchalchiuhtla ipan ye nicmatia nocuic aya ma yectlaxochitl y, zan nomac ton
mania, etc.

3. In quetzalin chalchiuhtla ipan ye nicmatia yectli ye
nocuic yectli noxochiuh annicuihuan tepilhuan aya
xonahuiacan a ayac onnemiz o in tlalticpac ayo.

4. O an niquitquiz ye niaz yectli nocuic yectli noxo-
chiuhui annicuihuan tepilhuan aya.

5. O huayanco o nichocaya a huayanco o cahua y
yahue nictzetzelo xochitl ay yo.

6. Mach nohuan tonyaz quennonamica o ah nicitquiz
xochitl zan nicuicanitl huiya ma yo a xonahuiyacan to ya
nemia ticaqui ye nocuic ahuaya.

7. Ay ca nichocaya nicuicanitl ya icha ahuicaloyan
cuicatl ha Mictlan temohuiloya yectliya xochitl onca ya
oncaa y yao ohuayan ca ya ilaca tziuhan ca na y yo.

8. Amo nequimilool amo neccuiltonol antepilhuan
aychaa ohuicaloyan cuicatl.

XXII.

*Tico, tico, ticoti, tico, tico, ticoti, and then the song ends
with totoco, totoco.*

1. In the place of tears I the singer watch my flowers;
they are in my hand; they intoxicate my soul and my
song, as I walk alone with them, with my sad soul among
them.

2. In this spot, where the herbage is like sweet ointment and green as the turquoise and emerald, I think
upon my song, holding the beauteous flowers in my
hand, etc. (as in v. 1).

3. In this spot of turquoise and emerald, I think upon
beauteous songs, beauteous flowers; let us rejoice now,
dear friends and children, for life is not long upon earth.

4. I shall hasten forth, I shall go to the sweet songs,
the sweet flowers, dear friends and children.

5. O he! I cried aloud; O he! I rained down flowers
as I left.

6. Let us go forth anywhere; I the singer shall find
and bring forth the flowers; let us be glad while we live;
listen to my song.

7. I the poet cry out a song for a place of joy, a
glorious song which descends to Mictlan, and there turns
about and comes forth again.

8. I seek neither vestment nor riches, O children, but
a song for a place of joy.

118   ANCIENT NAHUATL POEMS.

XXIII. *Ycuic Nezahualcoyotzin.*

*Totoco totoco tico, totoco totoco ic ontlantiuh tico titico ti tico
tico.*

1. Nicaya quetza con tohuehueuh aoniquimitotia
quauhtlocelo yn ca tiyayhcac in cuicaxochitl, nictemoan
cuicatl ye tonequimilol ayyo.

2. Ti Nopiltzi o ti Nezahualcoyotl o tiya Mictl a quen-
onamica y yece miyoncan ay yo.

3. Quiyon quiyon caya nichocaya ya ni Nezahualcoyotl huiya queni yeno yaz o ya nipolihuiz oya miquitla
ye nimitzcahua noteouh ypalnemo o tinechnahuatia ye
niaz nipolihuiz aya, yo.

4. Quenon maniz tlallin Acolihuacan huiya cuixoca
quen mano o ticmomoyahuaz in momacehuali ye nimitzcahua noteouh, etc.

5. Can yio cuicatli tonequimilol quipoloaya a in
totlacuiloli tepilhuan oo maya o huitihua nican aya ayac
ichan tlalticpac oo ticyacencahuazque huelic ye xochitl
ayio.

6. O ayae quitlamitaz monecuiltonol ypalnemoa a
noyolquimati cuelachic otictlanehuico Nezahualcoyotzin
ay oppatihua nican anaya y chan tlpc. Oon yn ay
oppatihua in tlalticpacqui, zan nicuicanitl ayaho onnicho-
caya niquelnamiqui Nezahualcoyotl aya ho.

7. Xo acico ye nican in teotl aya ypalnemoa, ayaho
on nichocaya a niquelnamiqui Nezalhuacoyotl ayio.

XXIII. *Songs of the Prince Nezahualcoyotl.*

Totoco, totoco, tico, totoco totoco, then it ends with tico titico, titico, tico.

1. I bring forth our drum that I may show the power and the grandeur in which thou standest, decked with flowers of song: I seek a song wherewith to drape thee, ah! oh!

2. Thou, my Lord, O thou Nezahualcoyotl, thou goest to Mictlan in some manner and at a fixed time, ere long.

3. For this, for this, I weep, I Nezahualcoyotl, inasmuch as I am to go, I am to be lost in death, I must leave thee; my God, the Giver of Life, thou commandest me, that I go forth, that I be lost, alas.

4. How shall the land of Acolhuacan remain, alas? How shall we, thy servants, spread abroad its fame? I must leave thee; my God, etc.

5. Even this song for thy draping may perish, which we have written for our children, it will no longer have a home here on earth when we shall wholly leave these fragrant flowers.

6. Alas! thy riches shall end; the Giver of Life teaches me that but for a little while do we enjoy the prince Nezahualcoyotl, nor a second time will he come to his house on earth; no second time will he rejoice on earth; but I the singer grieve, recalling to memory Nezahualcoyotl.

7. Let us seek while here the god, the Giver of Life; I grieve, recalling to memory Nezahualcoyotl.

XXIV.

Quititi, quititi, quiti tocoto, tocoti tocoto tocoti zan ic
mocueptiuh.

1. Ma xochicuicoya ma ichtoa nichuana ayyahue
teyhuinti xochitl ao ya noyehcoc ye nica poyoma
xahuallan timaliuhtihuitz ay yo.

2. Ma xochitl oyecoc ye nican ayyahue can tlaahui-
xochitla moyahuaya motzetzeloa ancazo yehuatl in nepa-
paxochitl ayyo.   Zan commoni huehuetl ma ya netotilo.

3. Yn quetzal poyomatl ayc ihcuilihuic noyol nicuicanitl in xochitl ayan tzetzelihui ya ancuel ni cuiya ma
xonahuacan ayio zan noyolitic ontlapanion cuicaxochitl
nicyamoyahuaya yxoochitla.

4. Cuicatl ya ninoquinilotehuaz in quemmanian xochineneliuhtiaz noyollo yehuan tepilhuan oonteteuctin in ca
yio.

5. Zan ye ic nichoca in quemanian zan nicaya ihtoa
noxochiteyo nocuicatoca nictlalitehuaz in quemanian
xochineneliuhtiaz, etc.

XXIV.

Quititi, quititi, quiti tocoto, tocoti, tocoto, tocoti, then it is to turn back again.

1. Let me pluck flowers, let me see them, let me gather the really intoxicating flowers; the flowers are ready, many colored, varied in hue, for our enjoyment.

2. The flowers are ready here in this retired spot, this spot of fragrant flowers, many sorts of flowers are poured down and scattered about; let the drum be ready for the dance.

3. I the singer take and pour down before you from my soul the beautiful poyomatl, not to be painted, and other flowers; let us rejoice, while I alone within my soul disclose the songs of flowers, and scatter them abroad in the place of flowers.

4. I shall leave my songs in order that sometime I may mingle the flowers of my heart with the children and the nobles.

5. I weep sometimes as I see that I must leave the earth and my flowers and songs, that sometime these flowers will be vain and useless.

XXV.

Tico toco tocoto ic ontlantiuh ticoto ticoto.

1. Toztliyan quechol nipa tlantinemia in tlallaicpac oquihuinti ye noyol ahua y ya i.

2. Ni quetzaltototl niyecoya ye iquiapan ycelteotl yxochiticpac nihueloncuica oo nicuicaihtoa paqui ye noyol ahuay.

3. Xochiatl in pozontimania in tlallaicpac oquihuinti ye noyol ahua.

4. Ninochoquilia niquinotlamati ayac in chan oo tlallicpac ahua.

5. Zan niquittoaya ye ni Mexicatl mani ya huiya nohtlatoca tequantepec ni yahui polihuin chittepehua a ya ye choca in tequantepehua o huaye.

6. Ma ca qualania nohueyotehua Mexicatli polihui chile.

7. Citlalin in popocaya ipan ye moteca y za ye polihui a zan ye xochitecatl ohuaye.

8. Zan ye chocaya amaxtecatl aya caye chocaya tequantepehua.

XXV.

Tico, toco, tocoto, and then it ends, ticoto, ticoto.

1. The sweet voiced quechol there, ruling the earth, has intoxicated my soul.

2. I am like the quetzal bird, I am created in the house of the one only God; I sing sweet songs among the flowers; I chant songs and rejoice in my heart.

3. The fuming dew-drops from the flowers in the field intoxicate my soul.

4. I grieve to myself that ever this dwelling on earth should end.

5. I foresaw, being a Mexican, that our rule began to be destroyed, I went forth weeping that it was to bow down and be destroyed.

6. Let me not be angry that the grandeur of Mexico is to be destroyed.

7. The smoking stars gather together against it; the one who cares for flowers is about to be destroyed.

8. He who cared for books wept, he wept for the beginning of the destruction.

XXVI.

Toto tiquiti tiquiti ic ontlantiuh tocotico tocoti toto titiqui
toto titiquiti.

1. Oya moquetz huel oon ma on netotilo teteuctin aya
ma onnetlanehuihuilo chalchihuitl on quetzali patlahuac,
ayac ichan tlalticpac, ayio zan nomac onmania ooo y
xochiuh aya ipalnemoa ma onnetlanehuilo chalchihuitl.

2. Oyohual in colinia o on in icelteotl ipalnemaa
Anahuac o onnemia noyol ayio.

3. In yancuica oncan quixima ipalnemoani ca ye
Nonoalco ahuilizapan i in teuctli yehua Nezahualpilli y
yece ye oncan aya in tlacoch tenanpan Atlixco ayio.

4. Zan momac otitemic motlahuan zomal a ica ticahuiltia icelteotl in teuctli yehua.

5. Y yeho aye icnotlamati noyollo, zan niNonoalcatl,
zan can nicolintototl o nocamapan aya Mexicatl in ca
yio.

6. On quetzal pipixauhtoc motlachinolxochiuh in
ipalnemoa zan ca nicolintototl, etc.

XXVI.

Toto tiquiti tiquiti, then it ends tocotico, tocoti toto titiqui toto titiquiti.

1. Come forth to the dance, ye lords, let there be abundance of turquoise and feathers; our dwelling on earth is not for long; only let the gods give me flowers to my hand, give me abundance of turquoises.

2. Come let us move in the dance in honor of the one only god, the Giver of Life, while my soul lives by the waters (*or*, in Anahuac).

3. The Giver of Life made known a new song after the lord Nezahualpilli entered the strongholds of Nonoalco and sped his arrows within the walls of Atlixco.

4. Thou hast filled thy plate and thy cup in thy hands and hast rejoiced in the one only God, the Lord.

5. Alas, how I am afflicted in my soul, I, a resident of Nonoalco; I am like a wild bird, my face is that of a Mexican.

6. The beauteous flowers of thy battles lie abundantly snowed down, O Giver of Life; I am like a wild bird, etc.

XXVII.

Toco toco tiqui tiqui ic ontlantiuh toco tico tocoti.

1. Ma ya pehualo ya nicuihua in ma ya on acico ye
nicaan aya oya yĕcoc yehuan Dios in cayio in ma ya ca
ya onahuilihuan tepilhuan a ayamo acico ya yehuan
Dios oncan titemoc yehuan Dios a oncan huel in oncan
tlacat y ye Yesu Cristo in ca yio.

2. In oncan tlahuizcalli milintimani mochan aya moxo-
chiuhaya Dios aya chalchiuhcueponi maquiztzetzelihui
onnetlamachtiloya in ca yio in oncan ya o nepapan
izhuayo moxochiuh aya Dios a.

3. Zan ye xochitl moyahua oo zan ca itlatol in
ipalnemoani o ontepan ye moteca anahuac ooica tic-
huelmana atl on yan tepetl ayio.

4. Zan temomac mania cemilhuitl in niman ye tehuatl
toconyaittoaya ipalnemoani.

XXVII.

Toco, toco, tiqui, tiqui, and then it ends toco, tico, tocoti.

1. Let my song be begun, let it spread abroad from here as far as God has created; may the children be glad, may it reach to God, there to God whom we seek, there where is Jesus Christ who was born.

2. There the dawn spreads widely over the fields, over thy house, and thy flowers, O God, blossom beauteous as emeralds; they rain down in wondrous showers, in that place of happiness; there alone may my flowers, of various leaves, be found, O God.

3. There the flowers are the words of the Giver of Life; they are upon the mountains and by the waters; we find them alike by the water and the mountain.

4. Our day is in thy hand, and soon we shall see thee, thou Giver of Life.

NOTES.

SONG I.

The song is an allegory, portraying the soul-life of the poet. By the flowers which he sets forth to seek, we are to understand the songs which he desires to compose. He asks himself where the poetic inspiration is to be sought, and the answer is the same as was given by Wordsworth, that it is to the grand and beautiful scenes of Nature that the poet must turn for the elevation of soul which will lift him to the sublimest heights of his art. But this exaltation bears with it the heavy penalty that it disqualifies for ordinary joys. As in medieval tales, he who had once been admitted to fairyland, could nevermore conquer his longing to return thither, so the poet longs for some other condition of existence where the divine spirit of song may forever lift him above the trials and the littleness of this earthly life.

There is no sign of Christian influence in the poem, and it is probably one handed down from a generation anterior to the Conquest.

1. The word *peuhcayotl* from *peua*, to begin, intimates that this was a song chanted at the beginning of a musical entertainment. The verses are longer, and the phraseology plainer than in many of those following. There is also an absence of interjections and lengthened vowels, all of which indicate that the time was slow, and the actions of the singer temperate, as was the custom at the beginning of a *baile*. (See Introd., p. 20.)

1. *Ninoyolnonotza*, a reflexive, frequentative form from *notza*, to think, to reflect, itself from the primitive radicle *no*, mind, common to both the Nahuatl and Maya languages. The syllable *yol* is for *yollotl*, heart, in its figurative sense of soul or mind. The combination of *yolnonotza* is not found in any of the dictionaries. The full sense is, " I am thinking by myself, in my heart."

ahuiaca, an adverbial form, usually means " pleasant-smelling," though in derivation it is from the verb *ahuia*, to be satisfied with.

quetzal, for *quetzalli*, a long, handsome blue feather from the quetzal bird, often used figuratively for anything beautiful or precious.

129

chalchiuh for *chalchiuitl*, the famous green-stone, jade or emerald, so highly prized by the Mexicans; often used figuratively
for anything noble, beautiful and esteemed.

huitzitzicatin, a word not found in the dictionaries, appears to
be from *tzitzilca*, to tremble, usually from cold, but here applied
to the tremulous motion of the humming bird as it hovers over a
flower.

zacuan, the yellow plumage of the zacuan bird, and from similarity of color here applied to the butterfly. The zacuan is
known to ornithologists as the *Oriolus dominicensis*. These
birds are remarkably gregarious, sometimes as many as a hundred nests being found in one tree (see Eduard Mühlenpfort,
Versuch einer getreuen Schilderung der Republik Mexiko, Bd. I,
p. 183).

acxoyatzinitzcanquauhtla; composed of *acxoyatl*, the wild
laurel; *tzinitzcan*, the native name of the *Trogon mexicanus*,
renowned for its beautiful plumage; *quauhtli*, a tree; and the
place-ending *tla*, meaning abundance.

tlauquecholxochiquauhtla; composed of *tlauquechol*, the native
name of the red, spoon-billed heron, *Platalea ajaja; xochitl*,
flower; *quauhtli*, tree; and the place-ending *tla*.

tonameyotoc, the root is the verb *tona*, to shine, to be warm;
tonatiuh, the sun; *tonameyotl*, a ray of the sun, etc. As warmth
and sunlight are the conditions of growth and fertility, many
derivatives from this root signify abundance, riches, etc.

mocehcemelquixtia; *mo* is the reflexive pronoun, 3d sing., often
used impersonally; *cehcemel*, is a reduplicated form of the numeral *ce*, one; it conveys the sense of entire, whole, perfect, and
is thus an interesting illustration of the tendency of the untu-
tored mind to associate the idea of unity with the notion of perfection; *quixtia* is the compulsive form of *quiza*, to go forth.

onechittitique; 3d person plural, preterit, of the causative form
of *itla*, to see; *ittitia*, to cause to see, to show; *nech*, me, accusa-
tive form of the pronoun.

nocuexanco; from *cuexantli*, the loose gown worn by the
natives, extending from the waist to the knees. Articles were
carried in it as in an apron; *no-cuexan-co*, my-gown-in, the terminal *tli* being dropped on suffixing the postposition.

tepilhuan; from *pilli*, boy, girl, child, young person, with the rel-
ative, indefinite, pronominal prefix *te*, and the pronominal plural
termination *huan*, to take which, *pilli* drops its last syllable, *li;*

hence, *te-pil-huan*, somebody's children, or in general, the young people. This word is of constant occurrence in the songs.

teteuctin, plural with reduplication of *teuctli*, a noble, a ruler, a lord. The singer addresses his audience by this respectful title.

2. *ixochicuicatzini; i*, poss. pron. 3d sing.; *xochitl*, flower; *cuicatl*, song; *tzin*, termination signifying reverence or affection; "their dear flower-songs."

yuhqui tepetl, etc. The echo in the Nahuatl tongue is called *tepeyolotl*, the heart or soul of the mountain (not in Simeon's *Dictionnaire*, but given by Tezozomoc, *Cronica Mexicana*, p. 202).

meyaquetzalatl; from *meya*, to flow slowly, to trickle; *quetzalli*, beautiful; *atl*, water.

xiuhtotoameyalli; the root *xiuh* meant originally green (or blue, as they were not distinguished apart); hence *xiuitl*, a leaf or plant, the green herbage; as where the Nahuas then were this was renewed annually, *xiuitl* came to mean a year; as a comet seems to have a bunch of fiery flames growing from it, this too was *xiuitl*, and a turquoise was called by the same term; in the present compound, it is employed adjectively; *xiuh-totol*, turquoise-bird, is the *Guiaca cerulea*, Linn.; *ameyalli*, from *atl*, water, *meya*, to trickle, and the noun ending.

mo-motla; to throw one's self, to dash one's self against something, etc.

centzontlatolli; literally, "four hundred speeches." The numeral four hundred was employed, like the Greek "myriad," to express vaguely any extraordinary number. The term may be rendered "the myriad-voiced," and was the common name of the mocking-bird, called by ornithologists *Turdus polyglottus*, *Calandria polyglotta*, and *Mimus polyglotta*.

coyoltototl, literally, "the rattle-bird," so called from its peculiar notes (*coyolli* = a rattle), is one of the *Tanegridae*, probably the *Piranga hepatica*.

ayacachicahuactimani; composed of *ayacachtli*, the rattle (see *ante*, page 24); and *icahuaca*, to sing (of birds); to the theme of this verb is added the connective syllable *ti*, and the verb *mani*, which, in such connection, indicates that the action of the former verb is expended over a large surface, broadly and widely (see Olmos, *Gram. de la Langue Nahuatl*, p. 155, where, however, the connective *ti* is erroneously taken for the pronoun *ti*).

hueltetozcatemique; composed of *huel*, good or well; *tetozca*, from *tozquitl*, the singing voice ; and *temo*, to let fall, to drop ; *que* is the plural verbal termination.

3. *ma n-amech-ellelti*, vetative causative from *elleloa*, to cause pain.

cactimotlalique, appears to be a compound of *caqui*, to listen, to hear, and *tlalia*, to seat, to place.

amohuampotzitzinhuan, a compound based on the pronoun of the second person plural, *amo*, the particle *po*, which means similarity or likeness, and the reduplicated reverential plural termination. The same particle *po*, appears a few lines later in *toquichpohuan ; potli* = comrade, compeer.

4. *Tepeitic*, from *tepetl*, mountain, *ititl*, belly, from which is derived the proposition *itic*, within, among. The term is applied to a ravine or sequestered valley.

5. *quauhtliya ocelotl*, the expression *quauhtli, ocelotl*, is of frequent occurrence in the ancient Nahuatl writers. The words mean literally " eagle, tiger." These were military titles applied to officers commanding small bodies of troops ; figuratively, the words mean control, power, and dignity ; also, bravery and virtue. Comp. Agustin de Vetancurt, *Teatro Mexicano*, Tratado II, cap. 3.

6. *in tloque in nahuaque ;* this expression, applied by the ancient Nahuas to the highest divinity, is attributed by some to Nezahualcoyotl (see above, p. 36). It is composed of two postpositions *tloc* and *nahaac*, and in the form given conveys the meaning " to whom are present and in whom are immanent all things having life." See Agustin de la Rosa, *Analisis de la Platica Mexicana sobre el Misterio de la Santisima Trinidad*, p. 11 (Guadalajara, 1871). The epithet was applied in heathen times to the supreme divinity Tonacateotl ; see the *Codex Telleriano-Remensis*, in Kingsborough's *Mexico*, Vol. VI, p. 107.

8. *ximoayan ;* this word does not appear in the dictionaries of Molina or Simeon, and is a proof, as is the sentiment of the whole verse, that the present poem belongs to a period previous to the Conquest. The term means "where all go to stay," and was the name of the principal realm of departed souls in the mythology of the ancient Nahuas. See Bartholome de Alva, *Confessionario en Lengua Mexicana*, fol. 13 (Mexico, 1634) ; Tezozomoc, *Cronica Mexicana*, cap. 55 ; D. G. Brinton ; *The Journey of the Soul* (in Aztec and Aryan Myths), Philadelphia, 1883.

yhuintia, causative form of *ihuinti*, to make drunk. The Nirvana of the Nahuas was for the soul to lie in dense smoke and darkness, filled with utter content, and free from all impressions ("en lo profundo de contento y obscuridad," Tezozomoc, *Cronica Mexicana*, cap. 55).

II.

On the signification of the titles given to this poem see the Introduction, § 3.

1. *yehuan Dios;* literally "who are God;" the introduction of the Spanish *Dios*, God, is in explanation of *in tloque in nahuaque;* so far from proving that this song is of late date, this vouches for its genuine ancient character, through the necessity for such explanation.

2. *nelhuayotl*, the essence or source of something, its true nature; probably from *nelli*, true.

teoquecholme; the prefix *teotl*, divine, is often added as an expression of admiration. Sahagun mentions the *teoquechol* as a bird of brilliant plumage.

III.

The poet recalls a recent attendance on the obsequies of an acquaintance, and seeks to divert his mind from the gloomy contemplation of death and the ephemeral character of mortal joys by urging his friend to join in the pleasure of the hour, and by suggesting the probability of an after life.

1. *xochicalco;* compounded of *xochitl*, flower; *calli*, house; and the postposition, *co*. The term was applied to any room decorated with flowers; here, to the mortuary chamber, which Tezozomoc tells us was decked with roses and brilliant feathers.

ipalnemohuani, literally "the one by whom life exists." The composition is *i*, possessive pronoun, third person, singular; *pal*, postposition, by; *nemoani*, singular of the present in *ni* of the impersonal form of the verb *nemi*, to live, with the meaning to do habitually that which the verb expresses. It is an ancient epithet applied to the highest divinity, and is found in the *Codex Telleriano-Remensis*, Kingsborough's *Mexico*, Vol. VI, p. 128, note.

tolquatectitlan, from *toloa*, to lower, to bow; *quatequia*, t. immerse the head; *tlan*, place ending. In the ancient funeral ceremonies the faces of the assistants were laved with holy water. On this rite see the note of Orozco y Berra to his edition of the *Cronica Mexicana* of Tezozomoc, p. 435 (Mexico, 1878).

xoyacaltitlan; from *xoyaui*, to spoil, to decay, whence *xoyauhqui*, rank, unpleasant, like the odor of decaying substances.

xochicopal tlenamactli, "the incense of sweet copal," which was burned in the funeral chamber (see Tezozomoc's description of the obsequies of Axayaca, *Cron. Mex.*, cap. 55).

2. The translation of this verse offers some special difficulties.

IV.

A poem of unusually rich metaphors is presented, with the title "A Song of the Mexicans, after the manner of the Otomis." It is a rhapsody, in which the bard sings his "faculty divine," and describes the intoxication of the poetic inspiration. It has every inherent mark of antiquity, and its thought is free from any tincture of European influence.

2. *miahuatototl*, literally, "the corn-silk bird," *miahua* being the term applied to the silk or tassel of the maize ear when in the milk. I have not found its scientific designation.

6. *poyomatl;* the poyomatli is described by Sahagun (*Hist. de la Nueva España*, Lib. X, cap. 24) as a species of rose, portions of which were used to fill the cane tubes or pipes used for smoking. He names it along with certain fungi employed for the same purpose, and it probably produced a narcotic effect.

V.

From the wording, this appears to be one of the lost songs of Nezahualcoyotl, either composed by him or sung before him. (See the Introduction, p. 35.) It is a funeral dirge, dwelling on the fact of universal and inevitable death, and the transitoriness of life. There is in it no hint of Christian consolation, no comfortable hope of happiness beyond the grave. Hence it dates, in all likelihood, from a period anterior to the arrival of the missionaries.

1. *tonequimilol;* I take this to be a derivative from *quimiloa*, to wrap up, especially, to shroud the dead, to wrap the corpse in its winding sheets, as was the custom of the ancient Mexicans.

The word, however, seems an archaic form, as it does not lend itself readily to analysis.

The expression *in Dios*, I explain as in the note to II, 1, and do not consider that it detracts from the authentic antiquity of the poem.

2. *yoyontzin;* on the significance of this appellation of Nezahualcoyotl, see Introduction, p. 35.

3. *ti Nezahualcoyotl;* "thou Nezahualcoyotl." The princely poet may have addressed himself in this expression, or we may suppose the song was chanted before him.

5. *Nopiltzin;* the reference is to Quetzalcoatl, the famous "fair God" of the Nahuas, and in myth, the last ruler of the Toltecs. See D. G. Brinton, *American Hero Myths* (Philadelphia, 1882). The term means "my beloved Lord." On Tezozomoc, see Introduction, p. 35.

6. The text of the latter part or refrain of verses 5 and 6 is corrupt, and my translation is doubtful.

VI.

Most of the poems in this collection are not assigned to any author, but this, and apparently the one following, are recorded as the compositions of Tetlapan Quetzanitzin. He is evidently the personage spoken of by Sahagun as "King of Tlacopan," as present with Montezuma on the occasion of his first interview with Cortez. Later in the struggle Tetlapan appears as the associate of Quauhtemoctzin, the "King of Mexico." (See Sahagun, *Hist. de la Nueva España*, Lib. XII, cap. 16 and 40.) M. Rémi Simeon explains the name to mean "he who deceives the people by magic;" deriving it from *quetza*, he places; *te*, the people, *tlepan*, on the fire. A simpler derivation seems to me possible from *tetlapanqui*, miner, or quarryman (literally, stonebreaker), and *quetzalli*, red; *quetzatzin*, the lord or master of the miners.

Both this and the following are war songs, and have marked similarity in thought and wording. The introduction of the Spanish *Dios* was doubtless substituted by the scribe, for the name of some native god of war, perhaps Huitzilopochtli.

1. *Aua;* this word I take to be a form of the interjection *yahue*, or, as Olmos gives it in his *Grammar, aa.*

2. *nepohualoyan ;* "the place of counting or reckoning," from *pohua,* to count. The reference is not clear, and the translation uncertain. In some parts of ancient Mexico they used in their accounting knotted cords of various colors, like the Peruvian *quipus.* These were called *nepohualtzitzin.*

4. This verse is remarkable for its sonorous phrases and the archaic forms of the words. Its translation offers considerable difficulty.

xontlachayan, I take to be an imperative form from *tlachia,* to look, with the euphonic *on.*

teoatl tlachinolli, literally "the divine water (*i. e.* blood), the burning," and the expression means war, battle. In one of his sermons Fray Juan Bautista describes the fall of Jericho in the words, *otlaltitechya in altepetl teuatl tlachinolli ye opoliuh,* and explains it, "the town was destroyed with fire and blood" (*Sermones en Lengua Mexicana,* p. 122). The word *tlachinolli* is from *chinoa,* to burn.

quetzalalpilo ; a compound of *quetzalli,* a beautiful feather, and *tlalpiloni,* the band which passed around the head to keep the hair in place.

5. *melchiquiuhticaya ;* "he who presented his breast," an imperfect, reflexive form. Molina gives *melchiquiuh petlauhqui,* with the translation *despechugado. Vocabulario Mexicana, s. v.*

VII.

The second specimen from the muse of Tetlapan Quetzanitzin is the noblest war song in the collection. It is an appeal to his friends to join in a foray to Chiapas. The intoxication of the battle field is compared to that produced by the strong white wine prepared from maguey, which was drunk only on solemn occasions. The bard likens the exhaustion of his fellow warriors from previous conflicts, to the stupor which follows a debauch, and he exhorts them to throw it aside.

1. *oamaxque, o,* pret. *am,* you, *axque,* 2d pl. pret. from *ay,* to do.

octicatl, apparently an old form from *octli,* the intoxicating beverage prepared from the maguey.

oanquique, 2d pl. pret. from *cui,* to take.

ohuican, a place of difficulty and danger.

The frequent addition of the terminal *o* in this and the succeeding verses is merely euphonic.

2. *teoatl tlachinolli ;* see note VI, 4.

in maquiztli tlazotetl, the beloved jewels, a phrase which indicates that the broken stones and splintered emeralds referred to are the young warriors who fall in battle, the pride of their parents' hearts, who are destroyed in the fight.

The *tizaoctli,* white wine (*tizatl,* chalk, hence white, and *octli,* wine), referred to in this passage, is said by Sahagun to have been drunk especially at the feast of the god Papaztac, one of the many gods of the wine cup. *Hist. de Nueva España.* Lib. II, App. Tezozomoc mentions it as handed to the mourners at funeral ceremonies. *Cronica Mexicana,* cap. 55.

3. *xochitlalticpacilhuicacpao ;* in this long compound of *xochitl,* flower, *tlalti,* earth, and *ilhuicatl,* sky, with various postpositions and the euphonic terminal *o,* the final *pa* gives the sense of location, towards, in the direction of.

chimalxochitl ; "the shield flower," the shield or buckler of the ancient warriors, ornamented with tassels and feathers, is not unaptly called the flower of war.

VIII.

The entire absence in this lament for the dead of any consolation drawn from Christian doctrines, points clearly to a date for its composition earlier than the teachings of the missionaries. Its cry of woe is hopeless, and the title attributes its authorship to one of the old chieftains, *tlatoani,* who held the power before the Spaniard arrived.

1. *quetzalhuahuaciuhtoque,* from *quetzalli, huaqui ; in teintoque,* the splinters ; the same simile is employed in VII, 2.

2. *ximoayan,* see note to I, 8. The occurrence of this term here and in verse 3 testifies to the fact of a composition outside of Christian influences.

IX.

The title does not necessarily mean that this song is a translation from the Otomi language, but merely that the time to which it was chanted was in the Otomi style; or, the term *Otomi* may

J

have reference to the military officer so called.   The word is perhaps a compound of *otli*, path, and *mitl*, arrow.

The bard sings the vanity of earthly pleasures, and the reality
of earthly pains; he exhorts himself and his hearers not to neglect
the duties of religion, and lauds his own skill in song, which he
compares to the sweet voices of melodious birds.   There is
nothing in the poem which reflects European influence.

1. *xotlacueponi ;* the meaning of this compound is obscure.   It
is not found in the dictionaries.

2. The terminal *o* is inserted several times in the passage to
express emotion and fill the metre.

mixitl tlapatl.   A phrase signifying the stupor or drunkenness
that comes from swallowing or smoking narcotic plants.   See
Olmos, *Grammaire de la Langue Nahuatl*, pp. 223, 228 ; *oquiqueo*
is from *i*, to drink, or *cui*, to take, the *o* terminal being euphonic.

X.

The poet expresses his grief that his songs all dwell on painful topics; he exhorts his hearers of the vanity of fame and
skill in handicrafts, and of the uncertainty of life; closing, he
appeals especially to those of Tezcuco and Atecpan to listen
and believe his warnings.

In spite of the introduction of the Spanish word *Dios*, and the
exhortation to " believe," in the last line, it is possible that the
substance of this song was due to purely native inspiration ; yet
it may have been, like Song XIX, one of those written at an
early period for the converts by the missionaries.

XI.

In a similar strain as in the last poem, the bard bewails the
briefness of human life and friendships.   He closes with an appeal
to the Master of Life, of whom no mortal tongue can speak in
worthy and appropriate terms.

6. *ihuiti*, apparently a form of *ihuintia*.

tonan ; the reference appears to be to *Tonantzin*, Our Mother,
otherwise known as Cihuacoatl, the Serpent Woman.   She was
the mythical mother of the human race, and dispensed afflictions

and adverse fortune. See Sahagun, *Hist. de la Nueva España*, Lib. I, cap. 6. The name is a proof of the antiquity of the poem, which is throughout in the spirit of the ancient religion.

XII.

As stated in the Introduction (§ 10), a note prefixed to this song introduces it as a translation from the Otomi into the Nahuatl tongue. It admirably illustrates the poetic flexibility of the Nahuatl.

3. *epoyhuayan*, from *epoalli*, sixty; *teoquauhtli ocelotl*, "divine eagles, tigers." These terms refer to the warriors bearing these titles.

tlazomaquiztetl, "beloved, precious stones," a figure of speech referring to the youths who go to war. The same or similar metaphors are used in previous songs.

5. The fifth and sixth verses present serious difficulties of construction which I do not flatter myself I have overcome.

XIII.

The inhabitants of Huexotzinco were in frequent strife with those of Mexico-Tenochtitlan, and on various occasions the latter captured many prisoners. The present poem is represented to be a composition of one of these prisoners when he and his companions were confined in Tlatilolco, one of the suburbs of Tenochtitlan. It breathes hatred against his captors and an ardent thirst for vengeance. The latest date at which I find captives from Huexotzinco detained in Mexico is 1511, and it is to this year, therefore, that I assign the composition of the poem.

5. *Atloyantepetl;* this name possibly means "the mountain of the place of the water-falcons" (*atl*, water; *tlatli*, falcon; *yan*, place-ending; *tepetl*, mountain). I have not found it in other writers. (See Index.)

8. *tlaylotlaqui;* Siméon, on the authority of Aubin, explains this term as the name of a tribe living near Tezcuco. In derivation it appears to be a term of contempt, "workers in filth or refuse," scum, offscourings. It also appears in Song XV.

10. The construction of this verse is so obscure, or the text so imperfect, that the translation is doubtful.

XIV.

This poem, chanted in 1551 before the Governor of Azcapotzalco, by Francisco Placido, a native of Huexotzinco, is a Christian song in the style and metre of the ancient poetry. See the
Introduction, p. 51.

　1. *impetlatl;* the ordinary meaning of *petlatl* is a mat or rug; it
is here to be taken in its figurative sense of power or authority,
chiefs and other prominent persons being provided with mats
at the councils, etc.

XV.

This extremely difficult composition seems to be a war song,
in which the bard refers to the traditional history of the Nahuas,
names some of their most prominent warriors, and incites his
hearers to deeds of prowess on the battle field. I do not claim
for my version more than a general correspondence to the
thought of the original. In several parts, especially verse 18,
the text is obviously defective.

　1. *tzihuactitlan;* "the land of the tzihuac bushes." The tzihuactli is a small kind of maguey which grows in rocky localities.
The tenth edifice of the great temple at Tenochtitlan was a wall
surrounding an artificial rockery planted with these bushes. Sahagun, who mentions this fact, adds that the name of this edifice
was *Teotlalpan*, which literally means "on holy ground." (*Hist.
de la Nueva España*, Lib. II, App.) The *mizquitl* is the common
Mimosa circinalis.

　Chicomoztoc; "at the Seven Caves," a famous locality in Mexican legend, and the supposed birthplace of their race.

　2. *Colhuacan* is probably for Acolhuacan; the early rulers of
the latter were of the blood of the Chichimec chiefs of the Tepanecas.

　4. *Hueytlalpan*, "at the ancient land," perhaps for Huetlapallan, a locality often referred to in the migration myths of the Nahuas.

　5. *Atloyan;* see note to XIII, 6.

　9. The ceiba and cypress trees were employed figuratively
to indicate protection and safeguard. See Olmos, *Gram. de la
Langue Nahuatl*, p. 211.

　12. On *tlailotlaqui*, see note to XIII, 8. The interjectional
appendages to this and the following verse are increased.

15. Tepeyacan was the name of a mountain on which before the Conquest was a temple dedicated to the "Mother of our Life," Tonantzin.

16. *tlapalcayocan*, "the place of shards," of broken pieces, *i. e.*, the field of battle.

19. The word *totomihuacan*, which has already occurred in vv. 3 and 7, I have translated as referring 'to the war captains of the Mexican armies, called *otomi* (see Bandelier, *On the Art of War of the Ancient Mexicans*, p. 117). I am quite open for correction however.

27. *in ipetl icpal;* in a translation of an ancient song, Ixtlilxochitl renders the expression *in ipetl icpal in teotl*, "en el trono y tribunal de Dios," *Historia Chichimeca*, cap. 32.

29. *Mictlan;* the place of departed souls in Aztec mythology.

XVI.

In this stirring war-song, the poet reproaches his friends for their lukewarmness in the love of battle. He reminds them that life is transitory, and the dead rise not again, and that the greatest joy of the brave is on the ringing field of fray where warriors win renown. It is in the spirit of the Scotch harper :—

> "'Twere worth ten years of peaceful life,
> One hour of such a day."

1. Each verse terminates with an interjectional refrain. The frequent introduction of the particle *on* is intended to add strength and gravity to the oration.

2. *oppan piltihua.* Compare this expression with that in v. 22, p. 44.

3. *xochimicohuayan*, should perhaps be translated, "where the captives to be immolated to the Gods are taken." The *xochimique*, "those destined to a flowery death" were the captives who were reserved for sacrifice to the gods. See Joan Bautista, *Sermonario en Lengua Mexicana*, p. 180.

4. *yaoxochimiquiztica*, "pertaining to the slaughter of the flowery war." This adjective refers to the peculiar institution of the "flowery war," *guerra florida*, which obtained among the ancient Mexicans. It appears to have been a contest without provocation, and merely for the display of prowess and to take

captives to supply the demand for human sacrifices in the religious rites. On this see Tezozomoc, *Cronica Mexicana*, cap. 96.

XVII.

In this long fragment—the closing strophes are missing in my MS.—the bard represents himself as a stranger appearing before the nobles of Huexotzinco at some festival. The first two verses appear to be addressed to him by the nobles. They ask him to bring forth his drum and sing. He begins with a laudation of the power of music, proceeds to praise the noble company present, and touches those regretful chords, so common in the Nahuatl poetry, which hint at the ephemeral nature of all joy and the certainty of death and oblivion. An appeal is made to the Master of Life who inspires the soul of the poet, and whose praises should be ever in mind.

The words *Dios* and *angelotin*, in verse 26th, indicate that the poem has received some "recension" by the Spanish copyist; but the general tone impresses me as quite aboriginal in character.

2. *quauhtlocelotl*, see note to I, 5.

3. In this verse, as frequently elsewhere, the syllable *ya* is introduced merely to complete the metre. Ordinarily it is the sign of the imperfect tense, and has other meanings (see the Vocabulary), but in many instances does not admit of translation.

8. *noncoati*, for *ni-on-coatl*, I am a guest.

18. The references in this verse are obscure, and I doubt if I have solved them.

20. "The house of spring;" compare the expression in v. 1, of Nezahualcoyotl's song, p. 42.

21. A long oration of Xicontecatl, lord of Tizatlan, may be found in Clavigero, *Hist. Antica di Messico*, Tom. III, p. 40. The expression *in camaxochitzin*, from *camatl*, mouth, *xochitl*, rose, flower, and the reverential *tzin*, is noteworthy.

24. *petlacoatl*, the centipede or scolopender ; from *petlatl*, mat, and *coatl*, serpent, as they are said to intertwine with each other, like the threads of a mat (Sahagun, Lib. XII, cap. 4).

XVIII.

At this portion of the MS. several poems are preceded by a line of syllables indicating their accompaniment on the teponaztli (see Introduction, p. 32).

The present number is one of the most noteworthy songs of the collection. It belongs to the ancient cyclus of Quetzalcoatl myths, and gives a brief relation of the destruction of Tollan and the departure and disappearance of the Light God, Quetzalcoatl Ce Acatl. As I have elsewhere collated this typical myth at length, and interpreted it according to the tenets of modern mythologic science, I shall not dwell upon it here (see D. G. Brinton, *American Hero Myths*, Phila., 1882).

The text of the poem is quite archaic, and presents many difficulties. But my translation, I think, gives the general sense correctly.

1. *huapalcalli;* literally, "the house constructed of beams." This name was applied to the chief temple of the Toltecs; the ruins of an ancient structure at Tollantzinco were pointed out at the time of the Conquest as those of this building (see Sahagun, *Hist. de la Nueva España*, Lib. X, cap. 29).

coatlaquetzalli; this edifice, said to have been left incomplete by Quetzalcoatl, when he forsook Tollan, had pillars in the form of a serpent, the head at the base, the tail at the top of the pillar. (See Orozco y Berra, *Hist. Antigua de Mexico*, Tom. III, pp. 30 and 46.) The structure is mentioned as follows in the *Anales de Cuauhtitlan:*—

"*Auhiniquac nemia Quetzalcoatl quitzintica, quipeuahtica iteocal quimaman coatlaquetzali ihuan amo quitzonquixti, amo quipantlaz.*"

"And when Quetzalcoatl was living, he began and commenced the temple of his which is the Coatlaquetzali (Serpent Plumes), and he did not finish it, he did not fully erect it."

Nacxitl Topiltzin, "Our Lord the four-footed." *Nacxitl* appears to have been the name of Quetzalcoatl, in his position as lord of the merchants. Compare Sahagun, ubi supra, Lib. I, cap. 19.

2. *Poyauhtecatl,* a volcano near Orizaba, mentioned by Sahagun.

Acallan, a province bordering on the Laguna de los Terminos. The myth reported that Quetzalcoatl journeyed to the shores of the Gulf about the isthmus of Tehuantepec and there disappeared.

3. *Nonohualco;* the reference is to the *cerro de Nonoalco.* which plays a part in the Quetzalcoatl myth. The words of the song are almost those of Tezcatlipoca when he is introduced to Quetzalcoatl. Asked whence he came, he replied, "Nihuitz in Nonohualcatepetl itzintla, etc." (*Anales de Cuauhtitlan*).

4. The occurrences alluded to are the marvels performed by Quetzalcoatl on his journey from Tulan. See my *American Hero Myths*, p. 115.

5. The departure of Quetzalcoatl was because he was ordered to repair to Tlapallan, supposed to be beyond Xicalanco.

8. *quinti*, for *iquintia;* the reference is to the magic draught given Quetzalcoatl by Tezcatlipoca.

9. *In tetl, in quahuitl;* literally, "stone and stick;" a very common phrase in Nahautl, to signify misfortunes.

XIX.

In this song we have avowedly a specimen of an early chant prepared probably by Bishop Zummarraga for the native converts. The accompaniment on the teponaztli is marked at the beginning. The language is noticeably different from the hymn to Quetzalcoatl just given (XVIII).

XX.

Another song of the antique Quetzalcoatl cyclus. It bewails the loss of Tulan, and the bard seeks in vain for any joyous theme to inspire his melody, reflecting on all that has bloomed in glory and now is gone forever.

3. *Tetl-quahitl;* see note to XVIII, 9.

XXI.

The occurrence to which this poem alludes took place about the year 1507. The chroniclers state that it was in the early period of the reign of Montezuma II, that the natives of Huexotzinco, at that time allies of the Mexicans, were severely harassed by the Tlascallans, and applied, not in vain, to their powerful suzerain to aid them. (See Tezozomoc, *Cronica Mexicana*, cap. 97.)

The poet does not appear to make a direct petition, but indirectly praises the grandeur of Montezuma and expresses his own ardent love for his native Huexotzinco. The song would appear to be used as a delicate prelude to the more serious negotiations. It is one of the few historical songs in the collection. From the references in verses 1 and 3 we infer that this singer held in his hand the painted book from which he recited the couplets. This may explain the presentation of the piece.

1. *huetzcani;* one who laughs, a jester, perhaps the designation of one who sang cheerful songs.

chalchiuhatlaquiquizcopa; a word of difficult analysis. I suspect an omission of an *l*, and that the compound includes *tlaquilqui*, one who fastens and puts together, a mason, etc.

5. The sense is that the warriors of Montezuma when on the field of battle, shine in their deeds like beautiful flowers in a field, and win lasting fame by their exploits.

mopopoyauhtoc. The grammarian Olmos explains the reflexive verb *mo-popoyauhtiuh* to signify "he leaves an honored memory of his exploits." See Siméon, *Dictionaire de la Langue Nahuatl,* sub voce.

7. *Huexotzinco atzalan;* "Huexotzinco amid the waters." This expression, repeated in verse 8, appears inappropriate to the town of Huexotzinco, which lies inland. In fact, the description in verse 7 applies to Tenochtitlan rather than the singer's own town. But the text does not admit this translation. Perhaps we should read "Huexotzinco and Atzalan," as there are yet two villages of that name in the state of Puebla (which embraced part of ancient Huexotzinco).

10. *petiatolini*, I have derived from *petlatl*, suspecting an error in transcription. The reference is to the rushes in the mat on which the singer stood.

XXII.

The ordinary sad burden of the Nahuatl poets is repeated with emphasis in this plaint. It is a variation of the Epicurean advice, "Eat, drink, and be merry, for to-morrow we die." Both the sentiment and the reference to Mictlan in verse 7, point it out as a production uninfluenced by Christian teaching.

7. The word *ahuicaloyan*, place of sweetness, would seem to be identical with *ohuicaloyan*, place of difficulty, in v. 8; I have regarded the latter as an error of transcription.

XXIII.

Although No. V. is probably one of the lost songs of Nezahual-coyotl, the present is the only one of the collection which is definitely attributed to him. The language is very archaic, and in the sentiment there is every mark of antiquity.

The text is apparently a dialogue, which was chanted as strophe and antistrophe, the one singer speaking for the King, the other for the bard himself.

The word *teotl* is used for divinity, and it is doubtless this word for which the copyists of some of the other songs have substituted the Spanish *Dios*, thus conveying an impression that the chants themselves were of late date.

The last verse, however, seems to be by one who lives after the time of the great poet-prince, and is calling him to memory.

XXIV.

It will be seen that there is a wearisome sameness in the theme of most of the short poems. Probably the bards followed conventional models, and feared for the popularity of their products, did they seek originality. Here again are the same delight in flowers and songs, and the same grief at the thought that all such joys are evanescent and that soon "death closes all."

I consider the poem one of undoubted antiquity and purely native in thought and language.

XXV.

The destruction of the Mexican state was heralded by a series of omens and prodigies which took place at various times during the ten years preceding the arrival of Cortes. They are carefully recorded by Sahagun, in the first chapter of the 12th book of his history. They included a comet, or "smoking star," as these were called in Nahuatl, and a bright flame in the East and Southeast, over the mountains, visible from midnight to daylight, for a year. This latter occurred in 1509. The song before us is a boding chant, referring to such prognostics, and drawing from them the inference that the existence of Mexico was doomed. It was

probably from just such songs that Sahagun derived his information.

1. *toztliyan*, I suppose from *tozquitl*, the singing voice, in the
locative; literally, "the quechol in the place of sweet-singing."

2. *iquiapan*, from *i*, possessive prefix, *quiauatl*, door, entrance,
house, *pan*, in.

5. An obscure verse; *tequantepec*, appears to be a textual error;
tequani, a ravenous beast, from *qua* to eat; *tepec*, a mountain;
but *tequantepehua* occurring twice later in the poem induces the
belief *tequani* should be taken in its figurative sense of affliction, destruction, and that *tepec* is an old verbal form.

7. *Xochitecatl*, "one who cares for flowers," is said by Sahagun
to have been the name applied to a woman doomed to sacrifice
to the divinities of the mountains (*Hist. Nueva España*, Lib. II,
cap. 13).

8. *amaxtecatl*, or *amoxtecatl*, as the MS. may read, from *amoxtli*,
a book.

XXVI.

This seems to be a song of victory to celebrate an attack upon
Atlixco by the ruler of Tezcuco, the famous Nezahualpilli. This
monarch died in 1516, and therefore the song must antedate this
period, if it is genuine. It has every intrinsic evidence of antiquity, and I think may justly be classed among those preserved
from a time anterior to the Conquest. According to the chro-
nologies preserved, the attack of Nezahualpilli upon Atlixco was
in the year XI *tochtli*, which corresponds to 1490, two years before
the discovery by Columbus (see Orozco y Berra, *Hist. Antigua
de Mexico*, Tom. III, p. 399).

XXVII.

My MS. closes with a Christian song in the style of the ancient
poetry. It is valuable as indicating the linguistic differences
between these later productions of the sixteenth century and
those earlier ones, such as XXVI, which I have not hesitated to
assign to an epoch before the Spaniards landed upon the shores
of New Spain.

VOCABULARY.

The Roman numerals refer to the songs, the Arabic to the verses, in which the word occurs. Abbreviations: *lit.*, literally; *ref.*, reflexive; *pret.*, preterit; *rev.*, reverential; *freq.*, frequentative; *post.*, postposition; *Span.*, a Spanish word.

A, *adv.* No, not, in comp.

A, *n.* For *atl*, water, in comp.; as *acalli*, water-house, *i. e.*, a boat.

A, *interj.* Oh! ah! placed after the word on which stress is laid.

Ac, *pron., interj.* Who?

Aca, *pron.* Some, any; somebody.

Acalli, *n.* A boat, of any kind.

Ach, *dubitative particle.* Indeed? is it not? etc.

Achitzinca, *adv.* A little while, a short time.

Achquen, *adv.* At what time? When?

Aci, *v.* To reach, to acquire.

Acohuetzi, *v.* To console, to make glad. I, 3.

Acoquiza, *v.* To lift up, to raise, to increase in dignity or power.

Acotlaza, *v.* To console.

Acxoyatl, *n.* The wild laurel.

Ahauia, *v.* To rejoice, take pleasure in; freq. of *ahuia*.

Ahuachia, *v.* To wet one's self, to bathe. VII, 4.

Ahuachtli, *n.* Dew, moisture.

Ahuehuetl, *n.* The cypress tree; *Cupressus disticha.*

Ahuia, *v.* To rejoice, to be joyful.

Ahuiac, *adj.* Agreeable, pleasant, sweet.

Ahuian, *adj.* Content, satisfied.

Ahuicpa, *adv.* From one place to another. III, 3.

Aic, *adv.* Never.

Altepetl, *n.* Town, city, citadel.

Amech, *pron. rel.* You, to you.

Ameyalli, *n.* A fountain, a stream; *lit.*, flowing water.

Amilli, *n.* Watered and arable land. XIV, 6.

149

Amo, *adv.* No, not; *amo ma*, no other; *amo zannen*, not in vain; *pron.*, you, yours.

Amoxpetlatl, *n.* Book-mat. See XIX, 3.

Amoxtecatl, *n.* See XXV, 8, note.

An, *pron.* You.

Ana, *v.* To take, to grasp, to seize.

Anahuia, *v.* To be dissatisfied.

Anca, *adv.* Of the kind that. XVII, 12.

Ane, *adv.* Hollo! in calling.

Angelotin, *n.* Angels. Span. XVII, 26.

Ano, *adv.* As little, neither.

Anozo, *conj.* Or, perhaps.

Aoc, *adv.* Not yet.

Apana, *v.* To clothe.

Apano, *v.* To ford, to cross water. XVIII, 2.

Aquen, *adv.* Nothing, in no manner.

Aquin, *pron.* Who? *in aquin*, he who.

At, *adv.* Perhaps, perchance.

Atayahuili, for *at aya ueli*. Not yet, not even.

Atihuelmati, *v.* Not to be well. IX, 3.

Atl, *n.* Water.

Atlamachtia, *v.* To praise one; *ref.*, to be proud.

Atle, *pron.* Nothing.

Atley, *in atley*. Without.

Atonauia, *v.* To have a fever, to be sick.

Auh, *conj.* And, even, also.

Axalli, *n.* Bar-sand, water-sand.

Ay, *v.* pret. *oax*. To do, to make.

Aya, *adv.* Not yet, not now.

Ayacachtli, *n.* A musical instrument. See p. 24.

Ayahuitl, *n.* Fog, mist, vapor.

Ayauh cozamalotl, *n.* The rainbow; *lit.*, "mist of water jewels."

Ayoc, *adv.* Already not. *Ayoctle*, nothing more.

Ayoquan, *adv.* Aoc-iuan. Nothing like it, unequaled. XVII, 17.

Ayoquic, *adv.* Nevermore. V, 6.

Azan, *adv.* Not a little, not a few.

Azo, *conj.* Or, perhaps, perchance.

Aztlacapalli, *n.* The tail feathers of a bird. XVII, 10.

C, *pron. rel.* He, her, it, him; *postpos.*, with, by, in, from, at.

Ca, *adv.* Already, yes, because, for, truly, only.

Ca, *v.* To be (in a place).

Ca, *postpos.* With, by, by means of.

Cacali, *v.* To discharge arrows.

Cacopa, *post.* Toward, towards.

Cahua, *v.* To leave, to let, to desert, to stop, to lay down.

Calaquia, *v.* To enter, to go in.

Calli, *n.* A house; in comp. *cal,* as *nocal,* my house.

Calmecac, *n.* A public school. p. 10.

Camapantli, *n.* The cheeks, the face. XXVI, 5.

Camatl, *n.* The mouth.

Campa, *adv.* Where, whither.

Can, *adv.* and *postpos.* Where.

Canauhtli, *n.* A duck. XXI, 9.

Canel, *adv.* Since, as, because.

Caqui, *v.* To hear, to listen to.

Catlehuatl, *pron.* Who? which? whoever, whatever.

Catqui, *v.* irreg. From *ca,* to be (in a place).

Cauhtehua, *v.* To leave a place.

Caxtlauitl, *n.* A kind of ochre. XVII, 10.

Ce, *adj.* and *art.* One, a, an.

Cece, or **Cecen,** *adj.* Each, every.

Cecemelquixtia, *v.* To come forth wholly, perfectly. I, 1.

Cecemeltia, *v. ref.* To rejoice, to feel glad.

Cecemeltic, *adj.* Complete, whole, entire.

Cecemmana, *v.* To disperse, to scatter.

Cehuia, *v.* To rest, to repose.

Cel. Sole only.

Celia, *v.* 1. To receive, to obtain. 2. To blossom, to bloom.

Cemanahuatl, *n.* The world, the universe.

Cemelle, *adv.* With peace or joy. Usually with a negative *aic cemelle,* never peacefully. XV, 18; XVI, 1.

Cemilhuiltilia, *v.* To detain one for a day.

Cemilhuitl, *n.* One day.

Cen, *adv.* Forever, for always; *cen yauh,* to go forever, to die.

Cenca, *adv.* Very much, exceedingly.

Cenci, *adv.* Elsewhere.

Cenquixtia, *v.* To select from, to pick from.

Centzontlatolli, *n.* The mocking bird, *Turdus polyglottus; lit.,* "the myriad-voiced."

Centzontli, *adj. num.* Four hundred, used for any large number.

Cepanoa, *v.* To unite, to join together.

Chalchiuhitl, *n.* The Mexican jade or green stone ; emerald
fig., green ; precious.

Chane, *n.* Inhabitant or resident of a place.

Chantli, *n.* A dwelling, a residence ; in comp., *chan.*

Chia, *v.* To wait, to expect.

Chialoni, *n.* That which is awaited or expected.

Chicahuac, *adj.* Strong, powerful.

Chichia, *v.* 1. To make bitter. 2. To obey. XIII, 9.

Chichina, *v.* To snuff up, imbibe, or suck up, especially the
odors of burning incense, through a tube. VII, 4; XVII, 10.

Chichinaquiliztli, *n.* Torment, pain, suffering.

Chihua, *v.* To make, to do, to happen ; *chihua in noyollo*, my
heart is troubled, I am pained.

Chimalli, *n.* The native shield or buckler. VI, 4.

Chitoni, *v.* To sparkle, to glitter.

Chitonia, *v.* To gain, to realize a profit. V, 4.

Chittolini, *v.* To bow down, to sink.

Choca, *v.* To cry (of animals and man).

Ciahui, *v.* To fatigue one's self, to tire.

Cihuacoatl, *n.* A magistrate of high rank ; *lit.*, " woman serpent."

Cihuatl, *n.* A woman.

Citlalin, *n.* A star.

Co, *postpos.* In, from.

Coa, or **Cohua,** *v.* To buy, to purchase.

Cochitia, *v.* To sleep.

Cocoa, *v.* To pain, to give pain.

Cocolia. *v.* To hate.

Cocoya, *v.* To be sick.

Cohuatl, or **Coatl,** *n.* A serpent ; a guest ; a twin ; the navel ; a
spade.

Cohuayotl, *n.* Buying, purchasing. V, 2.

Colli, *n.* Ancestor, forefather.

Coloa, *v.* To twist, to turn, to bend.

Comoni, *v.* To crackle (of a fire) ; to be turbulent (of people).
XXIV.

Con, *pron.* Some one ; comp. of *c* and *on.*

Copa, *postpos.* By, toward.

Copalli, *n.* Resin, gum copal.

Coyoua, *v.* To cry, to yell. XIII, 7.

Coyohuacan, *n.* The place of wolves. XIII, 10.

Coyoltototl, *n.* The coyol bird, *Piranga hepatica.*

Coyotl, *n.* The coyote, the Mexican wolf.

Cozcatia, *v.* To deck with golden chains. IV, 4.

Cozcatl, *n.* Jewel, precious stone; a string of such; a chain or collar.

Cuecuexantia, *v.* To gather in the folds of the robe.

Cuecueya, *v.* To move to and fro. XXI, 9.

Cuepa, *v.* To turn, to return, to bring back.

Cueponi, *v.* To blossom, to bud, to bloom.

Cuetlani, *v.* To wilt, to perish. XV, 15.

Cuetzpalti, *v.* To act as a glutton, to revel in. XVII, 5.

Cuexantli, *n.* Gown, robe, petticoat.

Cui, *v.* To take, to gather, to collect.

Cuica, *n.* A song, a poem.

Cuicani, *n.* A singer, a poet.

Cuicoyan, *n.* A place for singing. See note to p. 10.

Cuihua, *v.* Pass. of *cui*, q. v.

Cuilia, *v.* Rev. of *cui*, q. v.

Cuiloa, *v.* To paint, to write.

Cuiltonoa, *v.* To be rich; to rejoice greatly; to enrich or cause joy. XV, 6.

Cuitlatl, *n.* Excrement, dung.

Cuix, *adv.* An interrogative particle.

Ecacehuaztli, *n.* A fan.

Ehecatl, *n.* Wind, air.

Ehecayo, *adj.* Full of wind, stormy.

Ehua, *v.* To lift up, especially to raise the voice in singing.

Elchiquihuitl, *n.* The breast, the stomach.

Elchiquiuheua, *v.* To fatigue, to tire. VI, 5.

Elcicihuiliztli, *n.* A sigh, a groan.

Elehuia, *v.* To desire ardently, to covet.

Ellaquahua, *v.* To animate, to inspire.

Ellelaci, *v.* To suffer great pain.

Ellelli, *n.* Suffering, pain.

Ellelquixtia, *v.* To cause joy, to make glad.

Elleltia, *v.* *Ref.*, to regret, to repent, to abstain; *act.*, to prevent, to hinder, to impede, to cause pain.

Epoalli, *adj. num.* Sixty

Eztli, *n.* Blood.

K

Huahuaqui, *v.* To dry up, to wither wholly. VIII, 1.

Hual, *adv.* Hither, toward this place.

Huallauh, *v. irreg.* To come hither.

Huan, *postpos.* In company with; also, a plural termination.

Huapalcalli, *n.* Houses of planks. See XVIII, 1.

Huaqui, *v.* To dry up, to wither.

Huecapan, *adj.* Lofty.

Huecatlan, *adj.* Deep, profound.

Huehuetl, *n.* A drum. See page 22.

Huehuetzi, *v. freq.* To fall often.

Hueiyotl, *n.* Greatness, grandeur.

Huel, *adv.* Well, good, pleasant.

Huelic, *adj.* Sweet, pleasant, fragrant.

Huelmana, *v.* To make smooth, or even; to polish, to burnish.

Huetzcani, *n.* A jester, a laugher. XXI, 1.

Huetzi, *v.* To fall.

Huetztoc, *v.* To be stretched out, to be in bed.

Huey, *adj.* Great, large.

Hueyatlan, *n.* Place of increase, from *hueya*, to grow greater.

Huic, *postpos.* Toward, against.

Huica, *v.* To accompany; to carry off; to govern, to rule, to direct.

Huihuica, *v.* To follow in crowds, or often.

Huihuitequi, *v.* To gather, to pluck.

Huilohuayan, *n.* Bourne, goal, terminus; from *huiloa*, all go.

Huipana, *v.* To put in order, to arrange.

Huitomi, *v.* To split, to fall. XVIII, 4.

Huitz, *v.* To come.

Huitzitzicatin, *n.* The humming bird. I, 1.

Huitzitzilin, *n.* The humming bird, *Trochilus.*

Huitzli, *n.* A thorn, especially of the maguey.

Huitztlan, *n.* The south; *huitztlampa*, from or to the south.

I, *v.* Pret. *oic.* To drink.

I, *pron.* His, her, its, their.

Ic, *conj.* For, since, because; *prep.* With, towards, by, in; *adv.* Where? when? *zan ic*, as soon as, often, only, on purpose.

Ica, *post.* With him, her, it, etc.

Icâ, *adv.* Sometimes, occasionally.

Icac, *v.* To stand upright.

Icahuaca, *v.* To sing (of birds).

Icali, *v.* To war, to fight. VI, 5.

Icauhtli, *n.* Younger brother. VII, 2.

Icelia, *v.* To incite another, to devote one's self to.

Icnelia, *v.* To do good, to benefit.

Icniuhtli, *n.* A friend, a companion; *tocnihuan*, our friends.

Icnopillahuelilocati, *v.* To be ungrateful.

Icnotlamachtia, *v.* To excite compassion.

Icpac, *postpos.* Upon, over.

Ihuan, *conj.* And, also.

Ihui, *adv.* Of this kind, in this way.

Ihuinti, *v.* To intoxicate, to make drunk.

Ihuitl, *n.* Feather, plumage.

Ilacatziui, *v.* To twist, to twine.

Ilacatzoa, *v.* To twine around, to wind about. XV, 2.

Ilcahua, *v.* To forget.

Ilhuia, *v.* To speak, to say, to tell.

Ilhuicatl, *n.* Heaven, the sky.

Ilnamiquilia, *v.* To remember, to call to mind.

Ilpia, *v.* To bind, to fasten.

Im. See *in*.

Imati, *v.* To be skillful or wise; to prepare or arrange something skillfully.

In, *art. and pron.* He, they, the, which, etc.; *in ma oc*, meanwhile; *in ic*, so that, in order that.

Inaya, *v.* To confer, to hide. X, 2.

Inecui, *v.* To smell something, to perceive an odor. IV, 6.

Inic, *adv.* For, in order that, after that.

Inin, *pron.* These, they.

Iniquac, *conj.* When.

Inne, *conj.* But.

Inoc, *adv.* While, during.

Inon, *pron.* Those.

Intla, *conj.* If.

Intlacamo, *adv.* Unless, if not.

Ipalnemoani, *n.* A name of God. See III, 1, note.

Ipampa, *adv.* Because.

Ipotoctli, *n.* Smoke, vapor, exhalation.

Itauhcayotl, *n.* Fame, honor. XVII, 14.

Ithua, *v.* To see, for *itta*. XV, 6.

Itia, *v.* 1. To drink; to cause to drink. 2. To suit, to fit.

Itic, *postpos.* Within, inside of.

Itlani, *v.* To ask, to solicit, to demand.

Itoa, *v.* To say, to speak, to tell.

Itonaliztli, *n.* Sweat; *fig.*, hard work. VI, 5.

Itotia, *n.* To dance in the native fashion.

Itotiliztli, *n.* Dance.

Itta, *v.* To see, to behold.

Ittitia, *v.* To show, to make evident.

Itzmolini, *v.* To be born, to sprout, to grow. XX, 4.

Itztapalli, *n.* Paving stone. XV, 8.

Itztoc, *v.* To watch, to keep awake, to wait for. XVII, 12.

Ixamayo, *adj.* Known, recognized. XIII, 2.

Ixayotl, *n.* A tear (from the eyes).

Ixcuitia, *v.* To take example.

Iximachoca, *n.* The knowledge of a person.

Iximati, *v.* To know personally.

Ixitia, *v.* To awake, to arouse.

Ixpan, *postpos.* Before the face of, in presence of.

Ixquich, *adv.* As many as.

Ixtia, *v.* To face a person, especially the enemy; to watch.

Ixtlahuatl, *n.* Open field, savanna, desert.

Ixtlan, *postpos.* Before the face of.

Ixtli, *n.* Face, visage; eye.

Iza, *v.* To awaken, to arouse.

Izcali, *v.* To arise, to rise up.

Izhuatl, *n.* A leaf of a tree, etc.

Izhuayo, *adj.* Leafy, with leaves.

Izqui, *adj.*, *pl.* izquintin. As many, so many, all; *izqui in quezqui,*
    as many as.

Iztac, *adj.* White.

Iztlacahuia, *v.* To deceive, to cheat.

Iztlacoa, *v.* To search for; *ref.*, to take counsel.

Ma, *adv.* Sign of optative, subjunctive and vetative; *ma oc,* yet
    a while.

Maca, *v.* To give, to present.

Ma ca, *neg.* Do not.

Macaic, *adv.* Never.

Macazo tlein, *neg.* No matter, for all that. VI, 2.

Macehuallotl, *n.* Servitude, slavery.

Maceualti, *v. defect.* To merit; to be happy.

Macehualtia, *v.* 1. *nino*, to make another a vassal, to reduce to vassalage; *nite*, to give vassals to one; *nita*, to impose a penance on one.

Mach, *adv.* An intensive particle.

Machtia, *v.* To cause to know, to teach, to learn.

Maciui, *adv.* Although, granted that., XVII, 13.

Macquaitl, *n.* The native sword. VI, 4.

Macuele, *adv.* Would that—sign of the optative.

Mahaca, *adv.* Not, no.

Mahui, *v.* To fear, to have fear.

Mahuizti, *v.* To be esteemed, to be honored.

Maitl, *n.* The hand, the arm. In comp. *ma*, as *noma*, my hand.

Malacachoa, *v.* To twine, to fold. XVI, 4.

Malhuia, *v.* To regale, to treat well, to take care of.

Malina, *v.* To twine, to wreathe.

Malintiuh, *v.* To twine, to twist, to enwreathe.

Mamalia, *v.* To carry.

Mamalli, *v.* To enter, to penetrate. XII, 4.

Mamana, *v.* To arrange a feast, to set in order. XV, 15.

Mamani, *v.* See Mani.

Mana, *v.* To offer offerings. XVII, 3.

Manca, *v.* Imp. of *Mani.*

Manen, *neg.* That not, that it does not happen, etc.

Mani, *v.* To be (of broad or wide things); to be stretched out.

Manozo, *adv.* Or, if.

Maquiztli, *n.* A bracelet or other ornament of the arm. III, 5.

Mati, *v.* To know. *Ref.*, to think, to reflect; *qui-mati noyollo*, I presume, I doubt; *nonno-mati*, I attach myself to a person or thing.

Matiloa, *v.* To anoint, to rub.

Mazo, *adv.* Although.

Meya, *v.* To flow, to trickle.

Miahuatototl, *n.* A bird. IV, 2.

Micohuani, *adj.* Mortal, deadly.

Miec, *adv.* Much, many.

Milli, *n.* Cultivated field.

Miqui, *v.* To die, to kill.

Miquitlani, *v.* To desire death. X, 1.

Mitz, *pron.* Thee, to thee.

Mixitl, *n.* A narcotic plant. See *tlapatl.* IX, 2.

Mixtecomatl, *n.* A dark night, a dark place. III, 4.

Mizquitl, *n.* The mesquite. XV, 1.

Mo, *pron.* 1. Thy, thine; 2. *Pron. ref.* 3 sing., he, him, they, them.

Mochi, *adj.* All.

Mochipa, *adv.* Always.

Moliniani, *n.* One who moves, or agitates. XVI, 3.

Momolotza, *v.* To cause to foam, to cut to pieces. XII, 3.

Motelchiuh, *n.* The governor of Tenochtitlan. XIII, 8.—See *telchihua.*

Motla, *v.* To throw, to fall. I, 1.

Motlali, *adj.* Seated, placed, in repose.

Moyaua, *v.* To conquer; to become cloudy or troubled (of water); to talk about; to boast.

Moztla, *adv.* To-morrow.

Nahuac, *postpos.* Toward, by, along, near to.

Nahui, *adj. num.* Four.

Nalquixtia, *v.* To cause to penetrate, causative of *nalquiza*, to penetrate.

Nananquilia, *v.* To answer, to reply to.

Nantli, *n.* Mother, *tonan*, our mother, etc.

Nauhcampa, *adv.* In four directions, to four places.

Ne, *pron.* Reflexive pronoun 3d person in verbal substantives and impersonal verbs.

Ne, *pron.* for *nehuatl.* I, me.

Necaliztli, *n.* Battle, combat.

Nech, *pron.* Me, to me.

Nechca, *adv.* There, down there; like the French *là-bas; oc ye nechca*, formerly, once.

Neci, *v.* To appear, to show one's self or others.

Neco, *v.* Pass. of *nequi*, q. v.

Nectia, *v.* To desire, to wish for.

Necuiltonolli, *n.* Riches, possessions.

Neicaloloyan, *n.* The field of battle.

Neiximachoyan, *n.* A place where one is taught. XIII, 1.

Nel, *adv.* But.

Nelhuayotl, *n.* A root; *fig.*, principle, foundation, essence.

Nelihui, *adv.* It is thus, even thus; *mazo nelihui*, though it be thus.

Nelli, *adv.* Truly, verily.

Neloa, *v.* To mingle, to shake, to beat.

Neltia, *v.* To verify, to make true.

Nemactia, *v.* 1. To receive, to obtain. 2. To give, to grant.

Nemayan, *adv.* In the course of the year. XII, 3.

Nemi, *v.* To live, to dwell, to walk.

Nemoa, *v. impers.* To live, to dwell.

Nen, *adv.* Vainly, in vain.

Nenchiua, *v.* To do in vain.

Nenectia, *v.* To obtain by effort. XII, 4.

Neneliuhtica, *adj.* Mixed up, mingled together.

Neneloa, *v.* To mix, to mingle.

Nenepanoa, *v. freq.* To mix, to mingle. XVII, 1.

Nenequi, *v.* To act tyrannically; to feign; to covet. XI, 7.

Nennemi, *v.* To wander about.

Nenonotzalcuicatl, *n.* A song of exhortation.

Nentaci, *v.* To fail, to come to naught. XVII, 13, 14.

Nentlamachtia, *v. ref.* To afflict one's self, to torment one's self.

Nentlamati, *v.* To be afflicted, disconsolate.

Nepa, *adv.* Here, there. *Ye nepa,* a little further, beyond. XXI, 6. *Oc nepa,* further on.

Nepaniui, *v.* To join, to unite.

Nepantla, *postpos.* In the midst of.

Nepapan, *adj.* Various, diverse, different.

Nepohualoyan, *n.* The place where one is reckoned, read, or counted. VI, 2.

Nequi, *v.* To wish, to desire.

Netlamachtiliztli, *n.* Riches, property.

Netlamachtiloyan, *n.* A prosperous place. IV, 6; VII, 4.

Netlanehuihuia, *v.* To have an abundance of all things. XXVI, 1.

Netotiliztli, *n.* Dance, dancing.

Netotiloyan, *n.* Place of dancing.

Ni, *pron. pers.* I. Before a vowel, *n.*

Nican, *adj.* Here, hither.

Nihui, *adv.* From *no-ihui,* thus, of the same manner. XVIII, 3.

Niman, *adv.* Soon, promptly.

Nino, *pron. ref.* I myself.

Nipa, *adv.* Here, in this part, there.

No, *adv.* Also, like. *no yuh,* in the same way, thus. *Pron.* My, mine.

Noca, *pron.* For me, for my sake, by me.

Nohuan, *pron.* With me.

Nohuiampa, *adv.* In all directions, on all sides.

Nohuian, *adv.* Everywhere, on all sides.
Nonoyan, *n.* Place of residence. V, 2.
Nonotza, *v.* To consult, to take counsel, to reflect.
Notza, *v.* To call some one.
Nozan, *adv.* Even yet, and yet, to this day.

Obispo, *n.* Bishop. *Span.* XIX, 4.
Oc, *adv.* Yet, again; *oc achi,* yet a little; *oc achi ic,* yet more, comparative; *oc pe,* first, foremost.
Ocelotl, *n.* The tiger; a warrior so called. See note to I, 5.
Ocoxochitl, *n.* A fragrant mountain flower. III, 2.
Octicatl, *n.* See note to VII, 1.
Octli, *n.* The native wine from the maguey. In comp., *oc.*
Ohuaga, *interj.* Oh! alas!
Ohui, *adj.* Difficult, dangerous.
Ohuicaloyan, *n.* A difficult or dangerous place. XXII, 7.
Ohuican, *n.* A difficult or dangerous place.
Ome, *adj.* Two.
Omitl, *n.* A bone.
Ompa, *adv.* Where.
On, *adv.* A euphonic particle, sometimes indicating action at a distance, at other times generalizing the action of the verb.
Oncan, *adv.* There, thither.
Onoc, *v.* To be lying down.
Oppa, *adv.* A second time, twice.
Oquichtli, *n.* A male, a man.
Otli, *n.* Path, road, way.
Otomitl, *n.* An Otomi; a military officer so called.
Otoncuicatl, *n.* An Otomi song. II, 1.

Pachiui noyollo, *v.* I am content, satisfied. IX, 2.
Pacqui, *v.* To please, to delight.
Pactli, *n.* Pleasure, joy.
Pal, *postpos.* By, by means of.
Pampa, *postpos.* For, because.
Pan, *postpos.* Upon; *apan,* upon the water.
Papalotl, *n.* The butterfly.
Papaqui, *v.* To cause great joy.
Patiuhtli, *n.* Price, wages, reward.
Patlahuac, *adj.* Large, spacious.
Patlani, *v.* To fly.

Pehua, *v.* *Pret.*, *opeuh*, to begin, to commence.

Pepetlaca, *v.* To shine, to glitter.

Pepetlaquiltia, *v.* To cause to shine.

Petlacoatl, *n.* The scolopender, the centipede. XVII, 24.

Petlatl, *n.* A mat, a rug (of reeds or flags); *fig.*, power, authority.

Petlatotlin, *n.* A rush suitable to make mats. XXI, 10.

Petlaua, *v.* To polish, to rub to brightness.

Peuhcayotl, *n.* Beginning, commencement.

Pilihui, *v.* To fasten to, to mingle with. XXI.

Pilihuitl, *n.* Beloved child. XII, 3.

Pilli, *n.* Son, daughter, child. A noble, a chief, a ruler, a lord. *Tepilhuan*, the children, the young people. *Nopiltzin*, my lord.

Piloa, *v.* To hang down, to suspend.

Piltihua, *v.* To be a boy, to be young.

Pipixaui, *v.* To snow, to rain heavily.

Pixaui, *v.* To snow, to rain.

Pochotl, *n.* The ceiba tree; *fig.*, protector, chief.

Poctli, *n.* Smoke, vapor, fog, mist.

Poloa, *v.* To destroy; to perish.

Popoloa, *v.* Freq. of *poloa*.

Popoyauhtiuh, *v.* To leave a glorious memory. XXI, 5.

Poxahua, *v.* To work the soil, to labor.

Poyaua, *v.* To color, to dye. XVII, 21.

Poyaui, *v.* To become clear, to clear off.

Poyomatl, *n.* A flower like the rose. IV, 6.

Pozoni, *v.* To boil, to seethe; *fig.*, to be angry.

Qua, *v.* To eat.

Quahtla, *n.* Forest, woods.

Quahuitl, *n.* A tree; a stick; *fig.*, chastisement.

Quaitl, *n.* Head, top, summit.

Qualani, *v.* To anger, to irritate.

Qualli, *adj.* Good, pleasant.

Quatlapana, *v.* To break one's head; to suffer much.

Quauhtli, *n.* The eagle; a warrior so called; bravery, distinction. I, 5.

Quemach, *adv.* Is it possible!

Quemmach amique, *rel.* Those who are happy, the happy ones. IX, 2.

Quenami, *adv.* As, the same as.

Quenami can, *adv.* As there, the same as there, sometimes with *on* euphonic inserted, *quenonami.*

Quenin, *adj.* How, how much.

Quennel, *adv.* What is to be done ? What remedy ?

Quennonamican. See under *quenami.*

Quequentia, *v.* To clothe, to attire.

Quetza, *v.* *Nino,* to rise up ; to unite with ; to aid ; *nite,* to lift up.

Quetzalli, *n.* A beautiful feather; *fig.,* something precious or beautiful.

Quetzaltototl, *n.* A bird ; *Trogon pavoninus.*

Quexquich, *pron.* So many as, how much.

Qui, *pron. rel.* He, her, it, they, them.

Quiauatl, *n.* Entrance, door. XVII, 18.

Quiauitl, *n.* Rain, a shower.

Quimiloa, *v.* To wrap up, to clothe, to shroud the dead. XI, 6.

Quin, *pron. rel.* They, then.

Quiquinaca, *v.* To groan, to buzz, etc.

Quiquizoa, *v.* To ring bells. IV, 3.

Quiza, *v.* To go forth, to emerge.

Quizqui, *adj.* Separated, divided.

Quiztiquiza, *v.* To go forth hastily. XXII.

Tapalcayoa, *v.* To be full of potsherds and broken bits. XV, 16.

Tatli, *n.* and *v.* See p. 19.

Te, *pron. pers.* 1. Thou. 2. *Pron. rel. indef.* Somebody.

Teahuiaca, *adj.* Pleasing, agreeable.

Teca, *pron.* Of some one ; *te* and *ca.*

Teca, *v.* To stretch out, to sleep ; to concern one's self with. *Moteca,* they unite together.

Tech, *postpos.* In, upon, from. *Pron.* Us.

Tecocolia, *n.* A hated person, an enemy.

Tecomapiloa, *n.* A musical instrument. See p. 23.

Tecpilli, *n.* Nobleman, lord.

Tecpillotl, *n.* The nobility; noble bearing, courtesy.

Tehuan, *pron.* 1. We. 2. With some one.

Tehuatl, *pron.* Thou.

Teini, *v.* To break, to fracture.

Tel, *conj.* But, though.

Telchihua, *v.* To detest, to hate, to curse.

Tema, *v.* To place something somewhere.

Temachia, *v.* To have confidence in, to expect, to hope for.

Temi, *v.* To be filled, replete; to be stretched out. XXVI, 4.

Temiqui, *v.* To dream.

Temo, *v.* To descend, to let fall.

Temoa, *v.* To search, to seek.

Tenamitl, *n.* A town; the wall of a town.

Tenauac, *post.* With some one, near some one.

Tenmati, *v.* To be idle, negligent, unfortunate.

Tenquixtia, *v.* To speak forth, to pronounce, to declare.

Tenyotl, *n.* Fame, honor.

Teoatl, *n.* Divine water. See VI, 4, note.

Teocuitla, *n.* Gold, of gold.

Teohua, *n.* A priest. XVII, 19.

Teoquechol, *n.* A bird of beautiful plumage.

Teotl, *n.* God, divinity.

Teoxihuitl, *n.* Turquoise; *fig.*, relation, ruler, parent.

Tepacca, *adj.* Causing joy, pleasurable.

Tepeitic, *n.* Narrow valley, glade, glen.

Tepetl, *n.* A mountain, a hill.

Tepeua, *v.* To spread abroad, to scatter, to conquer. XV, 3.

Teponaztli, *n.* A drum. See p. 22.

Tepopoloani, *v.* To slay, to slaughter.

Tequani, *n.* A wild beast, a savage person.

Tequi, *v.* To cut.

Tetecuica, *v.* To make a loud noise, to thunder. XX, 7.

Tetl, *n.* A stone, a rock. In comp., *te.*

Tetlamachti, *n.* That which enriches, glorifies, or pleases.

Tetlaquauac, *adj.* Hard or strong as stone. Comp. of *tetl* and *tlaquauac.*

Tetozcatemo, *v.* To let fall or throw forth notes of singing. I, 2.

Tetzilacatl, *n.* A copper gong. XVII, 21. See p. 24.

Teuctli, *n.*, pl. *teteuctin.* A noble, a ruler, a lord; *in teteuctin,* the lords, the great ones.

Teucyotl, *n.* Nobility, lordship.

Teuh, *postpos.* Like, similar to.

Teuhyotl, *n.* Divinity, divineness.

Teyolquima, *adj.* Pleasing, odorous, sweet.

Teyotl, *n.* Fame, honor.

Ti, *pron.* 1. thou; *timo,* ref.; *tic,* act. 2. we; *tito,* ref.; *tic,* act.

Tilani, *v.* To draw out.

Tilini, *v.* To crowd, to press. XVII, 19.

Timaloa, *v.* To glorify, to exalt, to praise.

Timo, *pron. ref.* Thou thyself.

Tito, *pron. ref.* We ourselves.

Tizaitl, *n.* Chalk; anything white; an example or model.

Tizaoctli, *n.* White wine. See VII, 2.

Tla, *adv.*, for *intla*, if; *pron. indef.*, something, anything; *postpos.* in abundance.

Tlacace, *interj.* Expressing astonishment or admiration. XVII, 3.

Tlacaqui, *v.* To hear, to understand.

Tlacateuctli, *n.* A sovereign, a ruler.

Tlacati, *v.* To be born.

Tlacatl, *n.* Creature, person.

Tlacazo, *adv.* Truly, certainly.

Tlachia, *v.* To see, to look upon.

Tlachihual, *n.* Creature, invention.

Tlachinolli, *n.* Battle, war; from *chinoa*, to burn.

Tlacoa, *v.* To injure, to do evil, to sin.

Tlacochtli, *n.* The arrow.

Tlacocoa, *v.* To buy, to purchase. X, 1.

Tlacohua, *v.* To buy, to purchase.

Tlacohua, *v.* To beat, to chastise.

Tlacotli, *n.* A servant, slave.

Tlacouia, *v.* To split, to splinter.

Tlacuiloa, *v.* To inscribe, to paint in, to write down.

Tlaelehuiani, *adj.* Desirous of, anxious for.

Tlahuelli, *n.* Anger, ire.

Tlahuica, *n.* Servant, page; also, a native of the province of Tlahuican. (See *Index.*)

Tlailotlaqui, *n.* "Workers in filth;" scum; a term applied in contempt. XIII, 8; XV, 12, 14. Also a proper name. (See *Index.*)

Tlalaquia, *v.* To bury, to inter.

Tlalli, *n.* Earth, ground; *tlalticpac*, on the earth.

Tlalnamiqui, *v.* To think of, to remember.

Tlalpiloni, *n.* An ornament for the head. VI, 4, from *ilpia*.

Tlamachti, *v. ref.* To be rich, happy, prosperous.

Tlamahuizolli, *n.* Miracle, wonder.

Tlamatillolli, *n.* Ointment; anything rubbed in the hands. XI, 9.

Tlamatqui, *adj.* Skillful, adroit.

Tlamattica, *adj.* Calm, tranquil.

Tlamelauhcayotl, *n.* A plain or direct song. II, 1.

Tlami, *v.* To end, to finish, to come to an end.

Tlamomoyaua, *v.* To scatter, to destroy. XV, 21.

Tlan, *postpos.* Near to, among, at.

Tlaneci, *v.* To dawn, to become day. *Ye tlaneci*, the day breaks.

Tlanehuia, *v. Nicno.* To revel, to indulge one's self in. XXI, 8.

Tlaneltoca, *v.* To believe in, to have faith in.

Tlania, *v.* To recover one's self, to return within one's self.

Tlaniicza, *v.* To abase, to humble. IX, 3.

Tlantia, *v.* To terminate, to end.

Tlaocol, *adj.* Sad, melancholy, pitiful, merciful.

Tlaocolia, *v.* To be sad, etc.

Tlaocoltzatzia, *v.* To cry aloud with grief. I, 3.

Tlapalhuia, *v., rel.* To be brilliant or happy; *act.*, to salute a person; to paint something.

Tlapalli, *n.* and *adj.* Colored; dyed; red.

Tlapaloa, *v.* To salute, to greet.

Tlapanahuia, *adj.* Surpassing, superior, excellent; used to form superlatives.

Tlapani, *v.* To dye, to color. XVII, 10.

Tlapapalli, *adj.* Striped, in stripes.

Tlapatl, *n.* The castor-oil plant; the phrase *mixitl tlapatl* means stupor, intoxication. IX, 2.

Tlapepetlani, *v.* To sparkle, to shine forth.

Tlapitza, *v.* Fr. *pitza*, to play the flute. XVII, 26.

Tlaqualli, *n.* Food, eatables.

Tlaquauac, *adj.* Strong, hard.

Tlaquauh, *adj.* Strongly, forcibly.

Tlaquilla, *adj.* Stopped up, filled. XX, 4.

Tlaquilqui, *n.* One who plasters, a mason. XXI, 1.

Tlatemmati, *v.* To suffer afflictions.

Tlatenehua, *v.* To promise.

Tlathui, *v.* To dawn, to become light.

Tlatia, *v.* 1. To hide, to conceal; 2. to burn, to set on fire.

Tlatlamantitica, *adj.* Divided, separated.

Tlatlatoa, *v.* To speak much or frequently. XVII, 11.

Tlatlauhtia, *v.* To pray. XVI, 3.

Tlatoani, *n.* Ruler. lord.

Tlatocayotl, *n.* The quality of governing or ruling.

Tlatolli, *n.* Word, speech, order.

Tlatzihui, *v.* To neglect, to be negligent; to be abandoned, to lie fallow; to leave, to withdraw.

Tlauantli, *n.* Vase, cup. XXVI, 4.

Tlauhquechol, *n.* A bird, the red heron, *Platalea ajaja.*

Tlauillotl, *n.* Clearness, light. X, 1.

Tlaxillotia, *v.* To arrange, sustain, support. IX, 4.

Tlaxixinia, *v.* To disperse, to destroy.

Tlayaua, *v.* To make an encircling figure in dancing.

Tlayaualolli, *adj.* Encircled, surrounded. XXI, 6.

Tlaylotlaqui, *n.* See XIII, 8.

Tlayocolia, *v.* To make, to form, to invent. XIV.

Tlayocoyalli, *n.* Creature, invention.

Tlaza, *v.* To throw away; *fig.*, to reject, to despise.

Tlazotla, *v.* To love, to like.

Tle, *pron. int.* and *rel.* What? That.

Tleahua, *v.* To set on fire, to fire.

Tlein, *pron., int.* and *rel.* What? That.

Tleinmach, *adv.* Why? For what reason?

Tlenamactli, *n.* Incense burned to the gods. III, 1.

Tlepetztic, *adj.* Shining like fire, *tletl, petztic.* XV, 26.

Tletl, *n.* Fire.

Tleymach, *adv.* Why? Wherefore?

Tleyotl, *n.* Fame, honor.

Tlezannen, *adv.* To what good? Cui bono?

Tliliuhqui, *adj.* Black, brown.

Tliliui, *v.* To blacken, to paint black. XII, 6.

Tloc, *postpos.* With, near to.

Tloque nahuaque, *n.* A name of divinity. See I, 6, note.

To, *pron. posses.* Our, ours.

Toca, *v.* To follow.

Toci, *n.* "Our ancestress," a divinity so called.

Toco, *v.* Impers. of *toca.*

Tohuan, *pron.* With us.

Tolinia, *v.* To be poor, to be unfortunate.

Tolquatectitlan, *n.* The place where the head is bowed for lustration. III, 1.

Toma, *v.* To loosen, to untie, to open. XVII, 3.

Tomahuac, *adj.* Great, heavy, large.

Tonacati, *v.* To be prosperous or fertile.

Tonacatlalli, *n.* Rich or fertile land.

Tonameyo, *adj.* Shining like the sun, glittering.

Tonameyotl, *n.* Ray of the sun, light, brilliancy.

Tonatiuh, *n.* The sun.

Toneua, *v.* To suffer pain; *nite,* to inflict pain.

Toquichpohuan, *n.* Our equals. I, 3.

Tototl, *n.* A bird, generic term.

Tozmilini, *adj.* Sweet voiced. XXI, 3.

Toznenetl, *n.* A parrot, *Psittacus signatus.*

Tozquitl, *n.* The singing voice, p. 21.

Tzalan, *postpos.* Among, amid.

Tzatzia, *v.* To shout, to cry aloud.

Tzauhqui, *v.* To spin. XVII, 22.

Tzetzeliui, *v.* To rain, to snow; *fig.*, to pour down.

Tzihuac, *n.* A species of bush. XV, 1.

Tzimiquiliztli, *n.* Slaughter, death. XVI, 5.

Tzinitzcan, *n.* A bird, *Trogon Mexicanus.*

Tzitzilini, *n.* A bell.

Tzotzona, *v.* To strike the drum.

Uallauh, *v.* To come. See *huallauh.*

Uitz, *v.* To come.

Ulli, *n.* Caoutchouc. See p. 22.

Xahua, *v.* To paint one's self, to array one's self in the ancient manner. XXIV, 1.

Xamani, *v.* To break, to crack.

Xaxamatza, *v.* To cut in pieces, to break into bits.

Xayacatl, *n.* Face, mask.

Xelihui, *v.* To divide, to distribute.

Xexeloa, *v.* To divide, to distribute.

Xilotl, *n.* Ear of green corn.

Xiloxochitl, *n.* The flower of maize. XVII, 10.

Ximoayan, *n.* A place of departed souls. See I, 8.

Ximohuayan, *n.* Place of departed spirits. VIII, 1.

Xiuhtototl, *n.* A bird, *Guiaca cerulea.*

Xiuitl, *n.* A leaf, plant; year; anything green.

Xochicalli, *n.* A house for flowers, or adorned with them.

Xochimecatl, *n.* A rope or garland of flowers.

Xochimicohuayan, *n.* See XVI, 3, note.

Xochitecatl, *n.* See XXV, 7, note.

Xochitl, *n.* A flower, a rose.

Xochiyaotl, *n.* Flower-war. See XVI, 4, note.

Xocomiqui, *v.* To intoxicate, to become drunk.

Xocoya, *v.* To grow sour. XIII, 4.

Xopaleuac, *n.* Something very green.

Xopan, *n.* The springtime.

Xotla, *v.* To blossom, to flower; to warm, to inflame; to cut, to scratch, to saw.

Xoxoctic, *adj.* Green; blue. XVI, 6.

Xoyacaltitlan, *n.* The house or place of decay. III, 1.

Y. Abbrev. for *ihuan,* and *in,* q. v.

Ya, *adv.* Already, thus; same as *ye; v.,* to suit, to fit. Part. euphonic or expletive. See note to XVII, 3.

Yan, *postpos.* Suffix signifying place.

Yancuic, *adj.* New, fresh, recent.

Yancuican, *adv.* Newly, recently.

Yaotl, *n.* War, battle.

Yaoyotl, *n.* Warfare.

Yaqui, *adj.* Departed, gone, left for a place.

Yauh, *v., irreg.* To go.

Ye, *adv.* Already, thus; *ye no ceppa,* a second time; *ye ic,* already, it is already.

Ye, *pron.* He, those, etc.

Ye, *adj. num.* Three.

Yece, *adv.* But.

Yecen, *adv.* Finally, at last.

Yecnemi, *v.* To live righteously.

Yecoa, *v.* To do, to finish, to conclude.

Yectenehua, *v.* To bless, to speak well of.

Yectli, *adj.* Good, worthy, noble.

Yehuatl, *pron.* He, she, it. Pl. *yehuan, yehuantin.*

Yehuia, *v.* To beg, to ask charity.

Yeppa yuhqui. Formerly, it was there. VII, 2.

Yhuintia. See *ihuinti.*

Yocatl, *n.* Goods, possessions; *noyocauh,* my property. XV, 26.

Yocaua, *n.* Master, possessor, owner.

Yocolia, *v.* To form, to make.

Yocoya, *v.* To make, to invent, to create.

Yohuatli, *n.* Night, darkness.

Yolahuia, *v.* To rejoice greatly.

Yolciahuia, *v.* To please one's self, to make glad.

Yolcuecuechoa, *v.* To make the heart tremble. IV, 6.

Yolehua, *v.* To excite, to animate.

Yolihuayan, *n.* A place of living. III, 5.

Yollo, *adj.* Adroit, skillful; also for *iyollo,* his heart.

Yollotl, *v.* Heart, mind, soul.

Yolnonotza, *v.* See note to I, 1.

Yolpoxahua, *v.* To toil mentally.

Yuhqui, *adv.* As, like.

Yuhquimati, *v.* To understand, to realize.

Zacatl, *n.* Herbage, straw, hay. XXI, 5.

Zacuan, *n.* Feather of the zacuan bird; *fig.*, yellow; prized.

Zacuan tototl, *n.* The zacuan bird, *Oriolus dominicensis.*

Zan, *adv.* Only, but; *zan cuel,* in a short time; *zanen,* perhaps; *Zan nen,* in vain.

Zancuel achic, *adv.* A moment, an instant; often; *zan ye,* but again, but quickly.

Zanio, *pron.* I alone, he or it alone.

Zoa, *v.* To pierce; to spread out; to open; to sew; to string together; to put in order.

Zolin tototl, *n.* The quail.

Zoma, *v.* To become angry.

Zomale, *adj.* For *comalli,* vase, cup. XXVI, 4.

L

INDEX

171

the same radical as *iztac*, white, and, therefore, Father Duran was right in translating Aztlan, "place of whiteness," the reference being to the East, whence the Aztecs claim to have come. See Duran, *Historia de las Indias*, cap. II.

CACAMATL, 94, 95. The reference appears to be to Cacamatzin (the *Noble Sad One*, from *cacamaua*, fig. to be sad), last ruler of Tezcuco, son and successor, in 1516, of Nezahualpilli. He was put to death by Cortes.

CATOCIH, 89. A doubtful word, which may not be a proper name.

CHALCO, 16, 69, 95. A town and lake in the valley of Mexico. The people were Nahuas and subject to Mexico. The word is probably derived from *Challi*, with the postpos. *co*, meaning " at the mouth " (of a river). See Buschmann, *Ueber die Aztekischen Ortsnamen*, s. 689, and comp. *Codex Ramirez*, p. 18.

CHIAPA, CHIAPANECA, 70, 71. The province and inhabitants of Chiapas, in Southern Mexico. There were colonies of Nahuas in Chiapas, though most of the natives spoke other tongues. The derivation is probably from *chia*, a mucilaginous seed highly esteemed in Mexico.

CHICHIMECATL or CHICHIMECS, 88, 89, 91, 101. A rude hunting tribe, speaking Nahuatl, who settled, in early times, in the valley of Mexico. The name was said to be derived from *chichi*, a dog, on account of their de-

votion to hunting (*Cod. Ramirez*). Others say it was that of their first chieftain.

CHICOMOZTOC, 88, 89. "At the seven caves," the name of the mythical locality from which the seven Nahuatl tribes derived their origin. The *Codex Ramirez* explains the seven caves to mean the seven houses or lineages (totems) of which the nation consisted.

CHILILITLI, 36. Name of a tower of sacred import. It is apparently a compound of *chia* or *chielia*, to watch, and *tlilli*, blackness, obscurity, hence "a night watch-tower." It was probably used for the study of the sky at night.

CHIMALPOPOCA, 43. "The smoking shield," from *chimalli*, shield, and *popoca*. The name of several distinguished warriors and rulers in ancient Mexico.

CHOLULA or CHOLOLLAN, 105. Name of a celebrated ancient state and city. From *choloa*, with the probable meaning, "place of refuge," "place of the fugitives."

CIHUAPAN, 41. Name of a warrior, otherwise unknown. From *cihuatl*, woman, *pan*, among, with.

COATZITEUCTLI, 89. A name compound of *coatzin*, reverential form of *coatl*, serpent, and *teuctli*, lord.

COLHUA. A people of Nahuatl affinity, who dwelt in ancient times in the valley of Mexico. See *Colhuacan*.

COLHUACAN, 88, 89, 91. A town in the valley of Mexico. In spite of the arguments to the contrary, I believe the Colhua were of Nahuatl lineage, and that the name is derived from *colli*, ancestor; *colhua-can*, the residence of the ancestors; with this significance, it was applied to many localities. It must be distinguished from *Acolhuacan*. Its ikonomatic symbol was a hill bent over at the top, from *coloa*, to bend.

COLZAZTLI, 39. Probably for Coltzatztli, one who cries out or calls to the ancestors (*colli*, *tzatzia*). A chief whom I have not found elsewhere mentioned.

CONAHUATZIN, 41. A warrior not elsewhere mentioned. By derivation it means "noble son of the lord of the water" (*conetl, ahua, tzin*).

CUETZPALTZIN, 89. A proper name, from *cuetzpalli*, the 4th day of the month.

CUEXTLA, 33. A province of ancient Mexico. See Torquemada, *Monarquia Indiana*. Lib. II, caps. 53, 56.

CULTEPEC, 42. A village five leagues from Tezcuco, at the foot of the mountains. Deriv., *colli*, ancestor, *tepetl*, mountain or town, with postpos. *c;* "at the town of the ancestors."

HUETLALPAN or HUETLAPALLAN, 89. The original seat of the mythical Toltecs. The name is a compound of *hue*, old, and *Tlapallan*, q. v.

HUEXOTZINCO, 50, 83, 91, 99, 113. An independent State of ancient Anahuac, south of Tlascala and west of Cholula. The name means "at the little willow woods," being a diminutive from *huexatla*, place of willows.

HUITLALOTZIN, 89. From *huitlallotl*, a species of bird,

with the reverential termination. Name of a warrior.

HUITZILAPOCHTLI, 16. Tribal god of the Mexicans of Tenochtitlan. The name is usually derived from *huitzitzilin*, humming bird, and *opochtli*, left (*Cod. Ramirez*, p. 22), but more correctly from *huitztli*, the south, *iloa*, to turn, *opochtli*, the left hand, "the left hand turned toward the south," as this god directed the wanderings of the Mexicans southward. The humming bird was used as the "ikonomatic" symbol of the name.

HUITZILIHUITL, 89. "Humming-bird feather." Name of an ancient ruler of Mexico, and of other warriors.

HUITZNAHUACATL, 91. A ruler of Huexotlan (Clavigero); a member of the Huitznahua, residents of the quarters so called in Tezcuco and Tenochtitlan (Ixtlilxochitl, *Hist. Chichimeca*, cap. 38).

IXTLILXOCHITL, 35, 46, 89. A ruler of Acolhuacan, father of Nezahualcoyotl. Comp. *ixtli*, face, *tlilxochitl*, the vanilla (literally, the black flower).

IZTACCOYOTL, 89, 93. "The white wolf." Name of a warrior otherwise unknown.

MEXICANS, 67, 83, 85, 87, 123, 125. See

MEXICO, 83, 123. Name of the town and state otherwise called Tenochtitlan. *Mexitl* was one of the names of the national god Huitzilopochtli, and Mexico means "the place of Mexitl," indicating that the

rising from the valley of Mexico.

POYAUHTECATL, 105. A volcano near Orizaba (Sahagun. *Hist. de Nueva España*, Lib. I, cap. 21). Derived from *poyaua*, to color, to brighten.

QUANTZINTECOMATZIN, 41. A warrior not otherwise known. The name is a double reverential, from *quani*, eater, and *tecomatl*, vase, "The noble eater from the royal dish."

QUAUHQUECHOLLAN, 95. A village and plain near the southern base of Popocatepetl. It means "the place of the quechol woods," or the trees among which quechol birds are found. See Motolinia, *Historia de los Indios*, Trat. III, cap. 18.

QUAUHXILOTL, 89. Name of a large tree, and applied to a warrior, ruler of Iztapallocan, whom Ixtlilxochitl, King of Tezcuco, placed at the head of his troops in his war with Tezozomoc. See Clavigero, *Storia Antica di Messico*, Tom. I, p. 185.

QUETZALCOATL, 32, 143, 144. See note on p. 143.

QUETZALMAMATZIN, 91. Name of a warrior, "the noble one of the beautiful hands" (*quetzalli*, *mama*, pl. of *maitl*, and rev. term. *tzin*). Perhaps the same as Quetzalmemalitzin, ruler of Teotihuacan, mentioned by Ixtlilxochitl, *Historia Chichimeca*, cap. 35.

QUIAUHTZIN, 93. Name of a warrior, "The noble rain" (*quiauitl*, *tzin*).

TENOCHTITLAN, 85. The current name for the City of Mexico; literally, "at the stone-nopal," from *tetl*, stone, *nochtli*, nopal, and postpos., *tlan*. The term refers to an ancient tradition.

TEPANECAS or TECPANECAS, 35. A powerful nation of Nahuatl lineage, who dwelt in the valley of Mexico. They were destroyed in 1425 by the Acolhuas and Mexicans, and later the state of Tlacopan was formed from their remnants. Comp. probably from *tecpan*, a royal residence, with the gentile termination.

TEPEYACAC, TEPEYACAN, 93. From *tepetl*, mountain, *yacatl*, nose, point, and postpos., *c*. 1. A small mountain on which the celebrated church of the Virgin of Guadalupe now stands. 2. A large town and state subject to ancient Mexico, now Tepeaca in the province of Puebla.

TETLAPAN QUETZANITZIN, 68, 69. A ruler of Tlatilolco, contemporary of the conquest. See Note to Song VI.

TETZCOCO, now TEZCUCO, 14, 35, 36, 77. Capital city of Acolhuacan, and residence of Nezahualcoyotl. It has been called "the Athens of Anahuac." The derivation of the name is from a plant called *tetzculli* (*Cod. Ramirez*).

TEZOZOMOC, TEZOZOMOCTLI, 35, 39, 67, 88, 89. A ruler of the Tepanecas, celebrated for his warlike skill and severity. His death is placed in the year 1427. The name, like Montezuma, is derived from *zoma*, to be angry, in this case from the reduplicated frequentative form, *zozoma*.

TIZATLAN, 103. "The place of white varnish" (*tizatl*), the name of one of the four quarters of the city of Tlascala.

DATE DUE

NOV 27 '90			
APR 23 '9			
DEC. 5 1991			
APR 0 6 1992			
APR. 2 0 1992			
DEC. 1 5 1992			
MAY 0 7 1993			
MAR. 2 5 1994			
MAY 1 7 1995			
NOV 2 4 '96			
DEC 0 8 '9			
MAR 0 8 2002			
DEC 1 1 2006			
DEC 1 8 2012	ILL ⋇ 97307080 IAO		
GAYLORD			PRINTED IN U.S.A.